Creativity in Worship

Creativity in Worship

PAUL ALEXANDER

daybreak
London

First published in 1990 by
Daybreak
Darton, Longman and Todd Ltd
89 Lillie Road, London SW6 1UD

British Library Cataloguing in Publication Data

Alexander, Paul *1945–*
  Creativity in worship.
  1. Christian church. Worship
  Rn : William Alexander Smith I. Title
  264

  ISBN 0–232–51861–0

Phototypeset by Input Typesetting Ltd
London SW19 8DR
Printed and bound in Great Britain by
Courier International Ltd, Tiptree, Essex

Contents

Dedication

This book is about a fresh approach to God which is both completely new and yet as old as the human race. It is the approach of Creativity in Worship.

The earliest relics of the human race tell us that people have always engaged in worship which has always been creative in its expression.

The means and manner of expression go on changing and there have been periods in history when the flame of inspiration seems to have gone out.

This book is about keeping the flame lit.

The book is therefore dedicated to those outside the Christian Church in the hope that they might see something of the light.

It is dedicated to those inside the Christian Church, of whatever denomination, that they might keep the light burning.

It is dedicated to all sections of the Church that it may continue to nurture the Light of Christ.

It is dedicated to the organisation SEEDS, the creative resource service for the Church, that it may serve as a means of inspiring creativity within the Church (see p. 119).

The book is designed to serve as a guide for those embarking on the journey of creative worship.

It is a reference book for all those who find problems in some particular aspect of worship and it suggests means whereby such problems may be overcome.

It is an exploration of the dynamic force of worship which

re-awakens our sense of God's presence and encourages us to share it with others.

It is intended as an encouragement to church leaders and congregations who want to keep their worship alive.

It is an explanation, in imaginative terms, of the work of the SEEDS organisation.

SEEDS workshops have not only concentrated on the obvious artistic disciplines that can be employed within the Church but also new areas of creativity outside the normal concept of the arts such as counselling, prayer, parenthood, interview techniques and broadcasting.

But increasingly demand has come from within the Church for SEEDS artists to tackle the issue of Creativity in Worship which embraces all disciplines.

This book should encourage you to make use of the resource that SEEDS puts at your disposal.

It should encourage you to tackle the whole issue of Creativity in Worship for yourself.

We hope it will encourage you to do both.

1

Creativity and Worship

There is clearly an urgent need for a creative approach to worship, but if those who are thirsting after Heaven are to find an answer in the Church it is imperative that those already involved should at least be equally thirsty. Individually and corporately Christians of all denominations have been given a wonderful opportunity to work for the Kingdom of Heaven. This is an important task but not an easy one. In the book of Micah there is a vision of what the Kingdom of Heaven will be like where Peace, Love and Justice reign:

> In days to come where the temple stands will be the highest one of all, towering above all the hills. Many nations will come streaming to it and their people will say, 'Let us go up the hill of the Lord to the temple of Israel's God. He will teach us what he wants us to do; we will walk in the paths He has chosen.' For the Lord's teaching comes from Jerusalem; from Zion he speaks to His people. He will settle disputes among the nations, among the great powers near and far. They will hammer their swords into ploughs and their spears into pruning knives. Nations will never again go to war, never prepare for battle again. Everyone will live in peace among his own vineyards and fig trees, and no-one will make him afraid. The Lord Almighty has promised this. (4:1–4)

But we have to work for this vision with love, as the commandment says: 'We have to love the Lord our God with all our heart, with all our mind, with all our soul and with all our strength.' Jesus, in chapter thirteen of St John's Gospel, tells us what it means to love God when he says: 'A new commandment I give to you, that you love one another as I have loved you, by this shall all people know that you are my disciples if you have love one to another.'

Let's stand back a moment and look at ourselves. Twentieth-century men and women living two thousand years forward from Christ's day. How far have we come on the spiritual road that Jesus proclaimed as the way that leads to truth and everlasting life? Let's retreat from this world of ours for a while and look at ourselves in silence. What do we discover?

We are constantly being taken into the church, through radio services, television presentations and media publicity, and the impression we often get is of a group of stiff and starchy people looking awkward and seeming not to know each other too well. Is this purely media distortion or is there some truth in it? If it represents the truth in any way at all, what sort of image is that for the world to be receiving? No wonder the advertisements on television play a more prominent role in people's lives than religious broadcasting. If advertisements selling products, that the makers know in their hearts are superfluous, can persuade us that we need these products for our welfare, why can't the Church convince the world that what it has to offer is essential for our wellbeing? Does the Church propagate that what it has to offer is vital to our welfare?

At the time that Revelation was written John was challenging the church in Laodicea, and that challenge could easily be applied to many of our churches today. The church in Laodicea had become indifferent and apathetic to the challenge of Christianity. It needed to recover a vision of purity and joy. Today there doesn't seem to be enough genuine joy around in our churches, and by that I don't mean just jumping up and down, throwing our hands in the air and shouting 'Hallelujah'. I mean the sort of joy that has to be worked for, which transforms a dull and dying service into a service of celebration which proclaims that the Kingdom of Heaven is on hand.

If we find it difficult to work for Peace, Love and Justice, do we find it difficult to listen to God and to obey his Word? Do we find it difficult to turn our swords into ploughs and to love one another? If we do then the 'Church' should be there to help us and when members of a church group find it difficult to love each other – a far from infrequent occurrence – then 'individuals within the church' have the ordained responsibility to show what Christ's love means for others. 'I have chosen you and ordained you that you should go and bring forth fruit' (John 15:16), which means loving other people into life through Christ. But this love has to be expressed. It is a gift which we have been commanded by God to share with the world. We begin with self love, we move on to loving those who give things to us, we grow into loving those who show love and we mature further when we can love even those who don't love us. But how do we learn to express this vision of love to others?

Creativity in worship can be seen as a new way of appreciating what we already have and what we need. Its purpose is not to change the form, or other contents, if the form and contents are what the congregation wish to keep. It is a way of learning to re-evaluate, not only mentally but emotionally, physically and spiritually as well, what we have always taken for granted since what we take for granted so easily gets fossilised within our worship. Creativity in worship aims to fulfil the commandment, 'To love the Lord our God with all our heart, with all our mind, with all our soul and with all our strength and to love our neighbour as ourselves' (Luke 10:27). This is arrived at by understanding what happens during a service of worship, by asking the right questions, by using creative ways to explore those questions, by re-enacting the new-found truths that come to light as a result of these questions, and finally by reinjecting these discoveries back into the service. In this way the individual is led towards a deeper and more rewarding understanding of personal worship. This in turn leads towards a greater involvement in corporate worship; that gathering of individual worshippers, who, encouraged by a sense of creativity, are drawn together by its great unifying force.

The creativity of God is an infinite process in which we are all invited to participate. But we need to be aware that creativity involves upheaval. Creativity is a cyclical activity, just like the seasons. There is a time for apparent inactivity when the mind and body, soul and spirit are in a state of deep contemplation. There is a time of upheaval when the ideas are brought to birth. There is a time of fashioning when the ideas take shape, and there is the time for letting go so that the creation can come to maturity on its own.

There is a famous story about the discovery of the molecular structure of benzine. The scientist, Dr Friedrich Kekule, had been puzzling over it for many weeks without success. Then one night he dreamed about a serpent devouring its own tail, an ancient symbol of eternity. The structure which had eluded his waking mind had been revealed to him in sleep: the benzine molecule was a ring.

This story tells us a good deal about the nature of creativity. Creativity means putting the spiritual and the material together or harnassing the imagination to the physical in order to enliven, discover, devise and make. It is at work in cookery, personal relations, gardening, cleaning, repairing, in fact an endless range of the most ordinary of activities. It is a faculty which is inherent in all of us.

It is a mistake to think of some people as being naturally 'more creative' than others. Being creative is part of our God-given nature. But we can say that each of us is more creative in certain areas: it might be music or public speaking, coping with difficult people, or cooking a meal. And we can also say that in some the natural faculty of being creative is more developed.

There was a time when the Church recognised creativity for what it was worth and it is those results which have been living with us ever since, in art, music, sculpture, drama, and so on. But for far too long we have been living with a Church which shunned the help arts can give us and which has declined to express itself creatively. Part of the problem has always been that creativity involves effort. But thinking and acting in a creative way is not the prerogative of the artist alone, it belongs to everyone, from the story-teller to the baker of cakes. We are all creative beings, whether we like it or not, and it is to everyone's detriment when we cease to use our creative faculties. Creativity is the process of remoulding the new from the old.

We have all been given some of the power of God's own creativity and we have the freedom to exercise it as we will. However, when we discover this independence we are inclined to become intoxicated by it; we believe we can shine alone; we think we can become omnipotent. We want to reject God but retain his gifts. However we can use our creativity to reflect aspects of God. The Kingdom of God is within us and we must let it shine forth or it will perish for lack of use. The parable of the talents is an illustration of how failure to use our gifts stunts us and the parable of the light hid under the bushel is an illustration of how suffocation of our creativity leads to the extinction of the life within us. The revelation of God through people is a unique process. But we must relate to God. Just as a mirror cannot reflect sunlight unless it is pointed towards the sun, so we cannot reflect God's glory unless we are orientated towards him. The process of orientating ourselves in the direction of God is called worship.

The creativity of the human race can reflect God's glory and, as such, it is not merely a part of worship, there is a sense in which it is worship. Even in its most secular forms it can evoke the sacred in us. Childhood is usually full of such wonders because the creative faculty has not been suppressed. A sense of awe is not an illusion but an awareness of the underlying reality. Going to an art gallery 'may' bring a sense of the wonder and praise of God. But going to church 'ought' to revive the sense of the mystery of God and his creation. All too often it doesn't. The reason is that creativity is demanding. Creativity demands nothing less than one's whole self. It demands love which is the giving of one's whole being. It is incarnational. So we prefer to offer obedience. God does look for obedience but only when it springs from love. Therefore the role of creativity in Christianity is a central one because it helps the word come to life.

When a creative attitude is brought back into the heart of the Church it provides the most exciting way of approaching God and enjoying him. This applies as much to the coffee and cakes after the service as the stained glass window through which the sun shines during worship. The danger comes when these means are regarded as ends. When we cease to look through a window but simply at the glass, it stops being a window and becomes a wall.

Jesus said: 'I am the way' (John 14:6). The Christian life is one of voyage and discovery. As we take our tentative voyage of faith towards the true Paradise our creative gifts are needed to enable us to see clearly where we are going.

All Christians need to be involved in showing the world that Christianity is a creative force that has the power to realise our deepest needs and put us in touch with the experience of Heaven that is at the heart of all worship. This truth is alive, and it must be seen to be alive in the way we approach our worship creatively. We have to long to see God mirrored in every facet of our services, as the God of creation.

If Christianity is a living religion there can be no question that in order to be a part of it, in order to be able to go on calling ourselves 'Christian' we must involve ourselves in the outgoing life of the Church. If Christ says, 'Where two or three are gathered together, there am I in the midst of them' (Matt. 18:20), we must take his saying seriously. Christ is portrayed as outgoing, warm, friendly, caring particularly for the oppressed, the underprivileged, the sick and the poor. So we need to go further than the confines of the Church for the expression of our Christianity. Christianity is an outgoing religion.

People are seeking for truth but do not know where to find it. So we need to become beacons of light set on the hills and prophets of the reality of the Kingdom of Heaven. God only comes to us so that we might go to others. The creative life is quickly suffocated if we do not share our worship with the world. We must care about other people. We must care about all of life if we are to find fulfilment in God's creativity. The mistake we so often make is we think other people should be like us if they wish to share in what we have found. Other people are not like us, nor should they be. Helping a person towards holiness is a process of helping them to become what they were most truly created to be, lovers and worshippers of God.

Inspiration, a desire to search, sense, accept, learn, understand, respond, be involved, celebrate and reach out to the world – all these aspects of creativity are essential if we are to complete the pilgrimage to Paradise. For they are gifts of the Holy Spirit, who came upon the Church at Pentecost, and they are all expressed in our worship week by week, if we only know how to find them.

Worship is far greater than most of us allow it to be. Worship is three-dimensional. It is not a flat experience. We cannot distance ourselves from it and at the same time hope to be affected by it. It is an experience which reaches out to us and to which we are invited to respond. Our response draws us into the three-dimensional world of worship. It makes us whole because it connects us to the whole of God's creation. It is also three-directional and involves the worship of God, the worship of a person and the worship of a principle. These are common factors in all services of worship. The worship of God the creator of all things; the worship of Jesus Christ, the embodiment of God, and the worship of God's commandments, expressed in the principle that we should love one another as Jesus has loved us.

If the object of worship is three-dimensional, then its practice has to be too. There are common factors to the structure of worship and these factors apply to a general understanding of the word worship, not solely to the Christian understanding of it. The difference between various religions' interpretation of worship does not lie in the definition of worship itself but in the circumstances surrounding it. The interpretation of worship depends on the type, the background, and the culture of those who are worshipping. These may vary but the common factors that are inherent in the structure of worship remain.

The differences will appear in the diverse ways in which these common factors are used. If you study science you will understand this by thinking of worship as a prism. The source of light is God. The human beings standing on the other side of the prism perceive particular colours coming through depending upon which part of the spectrum they can see from where they are standing. The different people, standing in their different places, are the multi-denominational worshippers of God. An overall appreciation of God is made up of individual perceptions of these colours when combined together in worship.

No one has seen 'God' at any time, except Jesus. We perceive different 'facets' of God, knowing that all the time they are no more than images. We have the example of the perfect reflection of God in Jesus Christ. Our duty, and our joy, is to try to produce a reflection that comes as near as we can get to the perfect reflection of God as shown us by Jesus. That is the activity that Christians take upon themselves when they begin to worship God. It takes all sorts, all denominations, using the common factors of worship in varying combinations, to produce an overall picture of God's glory and even then we have only really begun to reflect a minute fraction of his true glory. This should not be a daunting or a depressing reality but a glorious, liberating fact that frees us to explore and express our love for the one who loves us beyond our deepest knowledge.

Why do we need to know what worship is? Why should we examine its structure? Wouldn't it be far better to leave it to the theologians and the clergy? Certainly not. If we fail to understand why worship provides a vital key to our happiness we are depriving ourselves needlessly. The more we understand the nature of worship the more we can give ourselves to God. We need to know why we are worshipping and we need to go on reminding ourselves of the reasons. Worship is the means by which we can draw nearer to God and therefore we are foolish if we do not want to know how it works.

Human beings come towards worship because they have experienced a glimpse of the glory of God and this has inspired them to start searching for him. Guided by God they discover the Church and then glimpse God again by sensing something of his presence in the devotion of the Church. When they have accepted that this is where they want to put down some roots they start to learn and to understand and to respond to the Church's worship of God. They become involved with the other people in the church, in celebration of all that God has revealed. Finally the worshipper comes full circle and the conclusion must be that he will want to share all that he has received, first of all in stewardship within the Church and then in outreach to the world beyond; in the same way that Christ came from the bosom of the Father and reached out to the world. If we take the trouble to understand the nature of worship and why we should involve ourselves in it, it will come alive for us in a most delightful way.

Understanding worship happens for us in many different ways. If we were all the same how dull this world would be, a monochrome grey like those drizzly days that leave one despairing of ever seeing the sun again. If we were all the same we would have absolutely nothing to offer each other. God loves each one of us, and his whole creation, with such passion that he wants us to love him for his own sake, but his love is not monochrome. It is full of a wonderfully colourful variety that comes to us through the huge diversity of gifts and talents with which he empowers us to return his love freely. If we all worshipped in the same way how dull it would be. We would be denying God our own unique reflection of his creation. We would be trying to minimise his splendour, which will always be beyond our boldest imaginings.

Nothing that God has created is lifeless. Everything that God creates is throbbing with life, even if we can't see it. Someone who has never come across a seed before would be forgiven for thinking that it was inanimate. Of course we know that this isn't the case. That apparently lifeless little seed is vibrant with life, if viewed in the right way. Its inherent life begins to show when it is seen for what it is, and treated accordingly. When it is given the right conditions in which to be creative it reveals its hidden potential and surprises us with its living beauty.

A denomination that wishes to make all other denominations like itself is doing God a huge disservice. It is refusing to acknowledge the Holy Spirit in all his fullness. It isn't the variety of denominations that matters; it is the acknowledgement of the two great commandments that matters. God has made each one of us unique in our ability to reflect the glory, the splendour, the majesty, the beauty and the love of God. For God's inspiration is endless. We have gifts that are unique to each of us and in sharing them is great joy. It is just the same with the things of the Spirit. There is a diversity of gifts but only one Giver. There is a diversity of churches but only one Cornerstone. There is a range of denominations but only one Leader. Our services of worship need to be different to reflect the endless facets of our Creator. For, in their diversity, they have one common goal, that of re-expressing our love for the God of all creation. So it is important to look at diverse types of worship from a non-denominational point of view.

On earth we have all kinds of churches with different types of architecture, interior design and varying traditions but they all profess the one Lord and the one belief in love. This love has to be shown especially to those who long to enter into, and feel at home with, the enduring Paradise of Heaven. Do we offer them, individually and corporately, in our different denominations, this reality, or do we offer them clichés, luke-warm friendship, because we ourselves have lost our desire for Heaven? To yearn for Heaven, for union with God, we must be people ceaselessly searching for and experiencing the Promised Land and trying to express its reality. This means offering up our talents and enthusiasms for the Kingdom of God in the service of our fellow human beings. Then our services will be transformed into acts of creative worship that will open the doors of heaven to all who wish to enter in.

2

Stages of Worship

There are twelve stages of worship that are passed through every time we worship God together. They can be summed up by the following words: **Inspiration** which is the desire for life; the awareness of the Holy Spirit and the sensation of God. **Searching** which is the longing to become whole; the desire to find the truth and a need to find God. **Sensing** which is the feeling for where truth lies; finding where God is and recognising God. **Accepting** which is agreeing to a set of values; conforming to a particular layout and settling down. **Learning** which involves following the word; studying the teaching and listening to God. **Understanding** which involves searching for the meaning; taking the teaching to heart and praying for enlightenment. **Responding** which involves reacting to God; acknowledging God and participating in worship. **Involvement** which includes sharing God with other people; helping each other and praying for others. **Celebration** which is a thanksgiving for the experience of God; a personal tribute and a mutual blessing. The **Conclusion** which is a recollection of God; a determination to follow God and a commitment to him. **Stewardship** which involves waiting on God in the church; serving the church in worship and serving the people in the church. And **Outreach** which involves taking one's experience of God out into the world; witnessing to God in the world and being a steward of God's world.

It is important for us to look at these twelve stages of worship if we want to bring our worship to life because if something is wrong our understanding will give us the ability to pinpoint where it is happening and to put it right.

Inspiration

Inspiration is the desire for life. When we lose our way in life we ask ourselves what are we doing, what are we looking for? We wonder if we will be in the dark forever? Can we find our way back to the light? Inspiration, that works in the heart of all of us, is there to tell us that we can and that it is possible to find our way back to meaning and enlightenment. It may not be easy to find meaning, but it is possible. Underneath, deep inside, everyone is inspired. What that inspiration is we may not have begun to put into words but it can be summed up as the desire for life.

This was vividly brought home to me many years ago when I used to spend all of my time potholing. One weekend I and a party of friends had gone to a slate quarry where we knew of a pothole which was going to be blasted the following week. The entrance was three quarters of the way up a cliff and the only way into it was from above. I volunteered to go down on the end of a rope and then throw a rope ladder from the pothole down to the ground.

I was wearing gym shoes which would grip on the slate. Very stupidly I let go of the rope before I was securely in the hole. I slipped and began to slide at increasing speed down the cliff. It was at about a forty-five degree angle and there was no way I could stop my descent.

At the bottom there was a fifteen-foot sheer drop and about ten feet from the edge of this was a pile of broken slate. I remember thinking that I had to keep going down feet first and to relax the moment that I hit the ground. I felt absolutely certain that my time had come.

It is true what they say. My life did flash before me. It made me realise that I desperately wanted to live with a sort of longing that I cannot describe. When I hit the ground I passed out. No bones were broken, but I was in shock for seventeen hours.

Something in those few brief moments had been uncovered, something which lies deep in all of us and is often only apparent in moments of extreme crisis. This is inspiration, not merely a will to live but a love of life for its own sake. It is a recognition of God's greatest gift; the awareness of the Holy Spirit. If we leave our inspiration only to these extreme moments we will hardly have lived. So we must place inspiration at the top of our list of priorities. It is the first and most vital step to rekindling our worship.

Perhaps we should be like children who write a shopping list of things they would like to receive from Father Christmas. Of course that list is likely to contain the glittering goods of this world but as soon as we learn that these things can never fully satisfy us we ought to progress onto the deeper level of asking for the things that really do satisfy us. For everyone that involves coming to terms with the meaning of their existence. Is there any point to it all? If we really believed there were no point to existence we would commit suicide.

With the threat of extinction, from nuclear warfare or the greenhouse effect, hanging over our heads we would be well advised to ask ourselves whether we do have reasons for living. There is no time to delay our response until tomorrow. If we start listening we will surely become aware of the Holy Spirit. We will sense the inspiration of God calling us towards a better world.

It is true that the first step has to be taken in faith and often in complete ignorance of the consequences. But our faith lies in the taking of that risk. This is not the sort of faith that blindly believes. It is the faith that is open to new possibilities. This sort of faith helps us find solutions because it springs from a desire for improvement.

Inspiration is the Holy Spirit of God waiting to be discovered inside us. It will provide us with all the answers we need to lead a fulfilled life. The important thing to realise is that inspiration exists in us.

If we faithfully follow our inspiration we will bring creativity to light. The realisation of the purpose for existence is a creative act. It takes time, energy and commitment to realise fully the beauty of hidden encounters with God and turn them into the open encounters which we experience in worship, and we have to refuel ourselves with the experience of these hidden encounters every time we go to worship because it acts as the catalyst for renewal. Our inspiration will open us up to a sensation of God. We must allow it to lead us into the light.

Searching

Once we have made up our mind to search, where do we start looking? There is no chance of finding what we are looking for unless we are guided from above. We may think we are doing the finding but in reality we are only doing the searching. The answers come but they rarely come when we expect them. It is a mysterious process. God is mysterious. We have to ensure that we have the eyes to see and the ears to hear, and to know that we have found what we are searching for when it arrives.

We are embarking on the greatest journey of our lives and we need to embark on this journey every time we venture to worship with others. We embark on a journey that many have trod before us. Their footsteps offer us only the barest indication of how we should go, but one thing is sure, countless people who have trodden the Christian path have spoken of the glory that lies before us. They have shown that they have indeed encountered the answers to our questions and that the encounter is good and makes us whole.

They have come from many different places and have entered the Church through many different doors but they have all encountered the true God through the life and example of Jesus Christ. We find the truth for our inspiration when we start searching for it in the life of the church. The truth is to be found in Christ, and Christ is found in the worship of the church.

Let us take a look at the nearest church available. One side looks very neglected, weeds are growing and there is an old broken gate, half off its hinges, padlocked to a rusty railing. The gate leads to a door which has peeling paint and a rusty handle and looks as though it hasn't been used for years. Above it there is a window with several holes in the glass giving us an impression of a derelict building but as we walk further round we see that there is some scaffolding around part of the roof which must indicate signs of life somewhere. Then we come across a notice-board, again peeling and tilting at an odd angle, but bearing a handwritten message offering salvation to all who enter in. It looks old and reminds one of those supermarket signs offering a twenty per cent discount off unsaleable goods.

Round the next corner we come across what is evidently a newish building in which there are obviously signs of life, but the atmosphere of the buildings hardly strikes us as welcoming.

And so we come round to the front of the building where there is another notice advertising the times of services and church personnel. This sign looks very imposing and gives us the impression of great efficiency. It is certainly clear and direct but there is still little feeling of a friendly welcome. However the church is obviously open and we decide to enter in.

As we approach the entrance certain questions begin to surface. Why are we here? Have we come because of curiosity? Is the church a place of historic interest to us or a place where, like a pub or a restaurant, we can gain a bit of refreshment? Is it sufficiently attractive for us to want to keep on returning for further refreshment, and what sort of refreshment does it offer anyway?

If we have a desire to meet with God these are the sort of questions we should ask ourselves because they help to clarify the degree of our commitment and focus our attention on how much we need to find God. We have come hoping for some inspiration that will open us to the possibility of saying 'yes' to a loving God. Suppose on entering we feel that our deepest longings will be fulfilled. Then our inspiration, our desire for life, will have led us to an experience that will keep us there. This is not an experience of the heavy hand of the law or of earthly power, but an experience akin to falling in love. Did we just stumble on this by sheer good luck or has the Spirit of God guided us there? This search to become whole, to find the truth of God, is a search we need to repeat every time we come to the church.

Now we are standing on the threshold of a new territory, momentarily overwhelmed. But we have a choice. If we allow ourselves to become involved we risk everything. If we deny our feelings it is because we fear they may lead us into the unknown. Love beckons us. We can enter in faith or turn back in ignorance. If we enter in faith we may be caught up in an experience where we are no more able to move than to cry out for joy. If we turn back our inspiration will have been denied. If we enter we may have to wait for some time before we are completely absorbed into the atmosphere because we will have to allow ourselves to be changed. We are not used to meeting God, so we have to give ourselves time to grow accustomed to his Spirit in that place.

Sensing

Standing on the threshold of the church, held by a sense of the unknown, uncertain of the feelings aroused, anxious to experience, what do we see? Great architecture, beautiful paintings, knights asleep in their armour? Inscriptions, brasses, banners? Wooden pews, rows of chairs? Rood screens, pulpits, altars, organs? Books, Bibles, stools, kneelers, notice-boards, maps, money boxes? These are just some of the things we may see on entering a church and they will strongly influence the way we react to the place.

Some churches place a strong emphasis on a musical tra-dition, others on a celebration of the arts. There are churches dedicated to promoting a certain aspect of the Christian mess-age, such as the passion, the resurrection or the Holy Spirit. There are churches dedicated to austerity or simplicity. There are churches that champion the military side of life or those lost at sea. There are churches that specialise in relics. There are those that concentrate on mystery and others that do not. There are many different opinions on how a church should function but it is always important that people feel at home with what they see, for this is the place where they hope to meet with God. It can be daunting to enter a place of worship. It can evoke all kinds of reactions. Some may feel it is a private place where they are unwelcome trespassers. It may appear to them to be a place that is full of irrelevant paraphernalia. The way a church looks is important not only for those who already worship there but also for newcomers. Sensing the creative presence of God in a church is important through all the stages of worship.

When Jesus talks about himself as the Vine and us as the branches he makes the point that without his Life being present in our lives we don't stand a chance of bringing forth any good fruit. Life in Jesus produces good fruit in abundance and the essence of that fruit is love. He tells us to rejoice in fulfilling this commandment of love. We must fill our churches with the expression of God's love. To dedicate our churches outwardly to the service of God and not inwardly fill them with Christ's love is to make a mockery of Christianity. The common factor all branches of the Church needs to express is love; practical down-to-earth love which can be seen and felt. It doesn't matter what stance our particular church takes within the Christian tradition. The worth of a church is the love it generates for the sake of its founder.

How does that love manifest itself to us?

I believe the answer lies in Jesus's saying, 'In my Father's house are many mansions . . . I go to prepare a place for you'

(John 14:2). The word mansions can be understood in several ways, such as dwelling places, rooms, staging posts, which indicate the idea of inns or hotels en route. All these words are associated with welcoming the stranger in. Our churches should follow this principle too. So the interior of a church, its layout and everything in it should create a feeling of welcome.

It's no good having a church layout which hampers people from being able to feel the presence of God or respond freely to his presence, that is counter-productive to every other stage of worship. So it is important to know what the relationship is between the layout of a church and its essential ingredient, which is the worship of God. The church's ideal is to make the presence of God so real that no one entering the building can fail to sense his presence.

However, sometimes, even under the most favourable conditions it is difficult to sense that God is present. Unless we spend time allowing ourselves to recognise that God is there, and tuning ourselves into his presence, the rest of our worship will have no real life in it. Our faith helps us to sense his presence if we give ourselves time.

If we call on the inspiration of the Holy Spirit, recognise the church as the place that makes us whole, and give ourselves time to sense the Spirit of God there before the collective part of our worship begins to take place, we are giving God the opportunity to present himself to us in worship that has the potential for being creative and alive. All we then have to do is accept his invitation and join in.

Accepting

To worship is to enter a mystery. Each time we decide to participate in a service we are committing ourselves to the unknown. If we are not searching for the way forward into greater depths of experience and understanding we are not partaking in worship, we are merely enacting a ritual. Ritual is a part of worship but it is not the whole of worship. When ritual becomes the dominating element of worship the result is sterility but when worship is creative it springs to life. Creativity is an explosive affair. We need to be prepared for its coming so that we can handle it when it arrives. How do we prepare ourselves for this creative life? Do we fervently pray that we won't be touched by it? Do we distract ourselves in various ways hoping that it will pass us by? Do we come thinking that worship is something which requires no effort or input from us? Do we come because it's the done thing or because we'll meet the right people? Do we come to sing, dance, or lose ourselves in emotion? Or do we come to learn more about, and enter more fully into, the life of God? Unless we desire to worship and concentrate on God, we are not really accepting him.

Love involves being able to ask, accept and absorb what we are given. We need to prepare ourselves for this opportunity. Jesus often retreated from the noise and bustle of everyday life into secluded places where he could listen attentively to the voice of God and converse with him in silence. This was his preparation for a ministry of love, and glorifying God. The church is the place, where we can come to God and find that space which is so essential if we are to accept the reality of his presence.

This requires a state of still acceptance. We have to learn to centre ourselves. We must let our minds rest in our hearts and in this attitude come before God. This should be practised every day in prayer, strengthened every Sunday in church, revitalised from time to time in retreat and perfected through our acceptance that God is all.

We need to meet God again every time we start our worship. We need to make sure that it is God who is put first in our worship and not ourselves. It is very easy to assume that because we know God is always with us that we are therefore always with God. It can often take a long time and much preparation to feel the presence of God. God does indeed want to speak to each one of us but only when we are ready to hear what he has to say. Worship has to do with listening.

The primary act of worship is adoration. To begin with adoration needs no words, no gestures, just acceptance. It is purely to be with God, to gaze on his face, to feel his love and to experience his protection. It is only when we have been absorbed into his goodness that it is truly possible to sing his praise, to rejoice in his word, and to ask for his favours.

But it may be that when we come into his presence we cannot gaze on his face or accept his love, because we are suffering deeply or think we don't deserve such love. It is sometimes as difficult for people to deal with total acceptance as it is with total rejection. The only way that a human being can honestly come before the presence of God is in a state of great humility which accepts the love of God unconditionally. The more honest we become, the more we know how far we fall short of what God wills us to be. But at the same time we always have the assurance that we have been totally accepted by God.

Love is the conferring of value on another: it cannot operate unless that value is recognised by both the giver and the one to whom it is given. So, if God declares us to be acceptable, who are we to say that we are unacceptable? Our mistake is not that we exaggerate our own value, but that we try to establish our value by means of false criteria, the estimation of this world rather than that of God.

Humble acceptance is not something to be scorned, it is something to be treasured because it leads us straight into God's presence. Jesus humbly accepted the most terrible death to point the way to God. Our humility is to accept who we really are, little people, far smaller than we spend most of our lives making ourselves out to be. Humility implies earthiness. *Humus* is of the earth, lowly, unnoticed and yet rich in potential. But the Bible reminds us, 'Dust thou art and to dust thou shalt return' (Gen. 3:19). It reminds us that our human condition is one of potentiality on earth and not one of fulfilment in this life. Humble acceptance is the recognition that we are nothing until we are aware that in God we have all our being.

Small wonder that Christ said it was harder for a rich man to enter the Kingdom of Heaven than for a camel to go through the eye of a needle. Accepting the cloak of humility may be painful to start with but in time it becomes a liberating experience which leads us towards self-knowledge. It makes us realise that we no longer have to pretend. We're free to accept God's love with joy. It is the first stage in our corporate worship which allows us to learn about God.

Learning

We cannot begin the formal part of our worship until we have reminded ourselves of why we have come there and what we are there for. We come in order to be nourished by God's Spirit. We come because we want to drink in the words, the emotions, the stimulation that worshipping God gives us. 'Except you eat my flesh and drink my blood you have no [spiritual] life in you' (John 6:53). If we fail to prepare for worship we will fail to be properly nourished by it.

Having passed through the stages of Inspiration, Searching, Sensing and Accepting we are now ready to start the communal, or formal, part of worship. These stages of worship are essential because they help to make us receptive to the creative movement of God's Spirit. And the way in which we communally open ourselves out to the Holy Spirit of God is as important as any other part of the service. It is the foundation stone for everything else that follows. Our introduction to learning about God is a supremely creative act. It starts us on the voyage of discovery.

What gives worship its vitality is its engagement with a particular theme. We have to discipline our attention onto a particular aspect of God. It is quite impossible for us to comprehend the whole of God for 'No person has seen God at any time' (John 1:18).

In worship a theme produces a narrative thread which holds our attention and allows us to learn, within a manageable compass, something of God. Just as the first sentence of a story can either prompt us to read on or to shut the book for ever, so the introduction to worship should offer us some of the thrill of a good overture.

Our introduction to worship should stimulate us to want to experience and learn about God. If God brings each day into existence, as though it were the first day of creation, and treats us to a never-ending display of surprises, we ought to learn how to mirror his creativity in the freshness of our worship. And the fact that a service has a regular pattern does not mean that it cannot be fresh and new.

If we are going to learn anything about God we need to frame it in a way that makes it possible for us to learn. Most people learn best through imaginative comparison. All of Jesus's parables are examples of this way of teaching; they are narrative stories that explore an imaginative theme and leave the listeners to make the comparisons for themselves. All Jesus's parables start with a theme. But Christ didn't only use parables to help people learn about God, he used every creative device available to him. 'The son can do nothing of himself but what he sees the Father do. Whatsoever things he does this also does the son likewise' (John 5:19). The explanation of a theme needs telling in as many different ways as possible if we are to learn about it because learning is not only an occupation of the mind. Worship involves the whole of ourselves and so learning involves the emotions just as much as the mind. That is why we use singing, movement, visual aids, drama, reading aloud, preaching, recitation, and so on, to help us get the message which the theme lays out for us. In John's Gospel the theme can be summed up in the words, 'Jesus is the Christ, the Son of God. If you believe this you have Life through his Name' (John 20:31). If that was all that needed to be said then the rest of John's Gospel would never have been written and our hearts would not have been stirred into responding to the love of God. Our own creative facilities would not have been brought into play by the huge array of imaginative comparisons that would have been presented to us by the rest of the story and through which we can follow the word, study the teaching and listen to God. Robin Green in his book *Only Connect* makes this point very clearly.

Understanding

How many times have you sat in a cold and draughty church listening to an unintelligible sermon? How many times have you felt yourself to be the witness of a gloomy and indecipherable ritual? Just the same sort of criticism could be levelled at a night out at the cinema or theatre that makes one feel more forlorn coming out than going in. Why does this happen? It happens because there has been a lack of creative desire to communicate a message. Communication is the vital link. Communication means communion, a word that is familiar to Christians. It conjures up the idea of intimacy, the intimacy that allows one person to know another better than they know themselves. Unless we have this desire to know and be known by God intimately it is impossible to understand what we have learnt during the course of our worship.

In order to know a person intimately the heart as well as the head needs to be functioning. The head without the heart produces sterility. The heart without the head produces sentimentality. Sterility is boring, sentimentality is slushy. But put the head and heart together and you have a powerful combination that can bring worship to life. Worship with no heart, no warmth, no colour, no imagination is cold; a hopeless atmosphere in which to cultivate the intimate understanding between God and men and women. Understanding, like a seed, needs to be nurtured with the right conditions for it to grow. On the other hand worship with no intelligence, no coherent thought process, is like a navigator without a compass. The heart and the head are indispensable to each other for the healthy balance that is a part of Christianity. John the intellectual lying on Jesus' breast, his head next to the heart of Jesus, was in a position to understand.

If we put our hearts as well as our heads into the worship of God we shall also come to understand something of God. If we are to understand what we are taught which means more than learning with the mind alone we need to adopt an atmosphere of prayerful listening and contemplative waiting on God's word. To listen to a good sermon and allow ourselves no time to digest it in silence is to reduce the effect of that sermon.

If we take the search for the meaning of our worship seriously we will search with the heart and with the mind – we must conquer our fear, allow ourselves to meet with the mystery of God's love and let ourselves respond creatively to it.

This creative process is a discipline. We are working on ourselves to the salvation of our souls. Salvation is the process whereby we are healed. Our wounded feelings and uneasy consciences are soothed through the understanding we gain through worship. For understanding worship is the process by which we discover God.

We cannot expect the world to see Christianity alive in us, let alone experience Christ's presence within, unless we participate fully in worship. To do this we must understand what we are about. In order to understand we must search. In order to find we must listen.

Responding

Have you heard the saying that genius is 'Ninety-nine per cent perspiration, one per cent inspiration'? It is a tiresome saying commonly uttered by those who neither perspire nor are inspired, but there is an element of truth in it. Inspiration is not something that is at one's beck and call, it has to be worked for. There are plenty of us who fool ourselves, and others too, into believing that we are inspired and filled with the Holy Spirit and that we have the answers, but it is our response to our worship that matters. If we don't respond to what we have learnt and understood our worship is not inspired.

The Pharisees displayed this lack of response. They informed the people that they had the answers and that the people should be like them but they failed to respond to their own teachings. Jesus called the Pharisees white-washed sepulchres full of outward show but inwardly dead. What a brilliant simile. They claimed that God had spoken to the prophet Moses in the Old Testament and that they were followers of Moses. They followed the rules and regulations laid down by him but they never tried to understand these laws with their hearts. Consequently when a man came along who did proclaim the truth from his heart they denounced him as a sinner. Yet he was fulfilling, by word and deed, every day of his working ministry, the Old Testament prophecies concerning the true Messiah.

Jesus denounced the vain repetitions of the Pharisees. Meaningless, thoughtless repetition is not response, it is an excuse to avoid the real work of being creative. There is a place for repetition. It is there to help us concentrate and to overcome our inertia to the work of responding to God.

But there comes a point when we need to jump in at the deep end.

It is difficult and uncomfortable learning to respond. It requires an inner revolution and who wants a revolution? It is easier to have a political revolution involving the transformation of other people's lives than to have a revolution inside ourselves. That is the mistake every political reform makes and that is why religion can be such an unpopular message. Personal revolution is a sweaty affair, like giving birth. Every time we involve ourselves in an act of worship we are challenged with potential revolution.

How do we react? Most of the time we do everything in our

power to avoid the challenge. We coast along and are thankful to get out of the church in one piece. But we fail to realise that we are coming out more dead than alive because when we avoid the creative challenge we leave ourselves unchanged. If we leave unchanged we leave in a worse state than when we went in because deep down we know that we haven't responded. We've wasted a chance of allowing the Holy Spirit to act in us. Once we realise this it is difficult not to be haunted by the fact. We then either turn our back on God, which is hell, or we suffer until we face up to the challenge, and respond. If we respond to the challenge we realise that our lives are going to change quite significantly. What is being offered to us is not some paltry gift that will lose its lustre, leaving us dissatisfied. What is on offer is the stuff of life. The action of the Holy Spirit is one of the greatest gifts that we can receive. Its fruits are quite plain for all to see. A shining face, a light in the eyes, a compassionate heart, a desire to help, a longing to love. Once we've seen, once we've experienced, life can never be quite the same again, if we respond. The world's goods are trifling by comparison. When we start responding to God, by reacting to the understanding of his word, we start to acknowledge him, publicly, by participating in worship with all of ourselves. This is the first step in reflecting our inner understanding of God outwardly. It is the starting-point from which our outreach to the world is built up. We respond to God by acting on the impulse of his Holy Spirit, using all our concentration, in a creative effort to interpret the understanding of his word. It matters not a jot how successful we are. The attempt is all. We are not performers acting for the benefit of a paying audience. We are people trying to put into action our love for God who has shown us the way to everlasting life. God delights in what we offer him when it is offered from the heart, and such response is always rewarded by God's Spirit making himself known to us.

Involvement

Responding to God is a personal thing, even when it takes place in the context of a service, because it is a creative reaction to what happens when the heart and mind are asked to reflect God's work. It has to be followed in communal worship by involvement, where we share our response to God with other people. It is a difficult stage of worship because it means being sensitive to other people as well as being bold with oneself. If we don't open our thoughts and feelings to others we remain isolated. If we force ourselves on other people we prevent them from being able to open themselves to us.

We have to involve ourselves in a step of faith. The knowledge that we are wanted, that we are loved and that we are able to love is a great help to our taking this step and Christians who have matured in practising their religion, have a responsibility to help those who are new to it. It's very easy to put them off.

Involvement is not easy to practise. We may remember as children how it took us a long time to be persuaded to go into the sea. The water seemed to be full of unknown terrors. It takes nerve to steel oneself into entering unfamiliar territory. Involvement requires a willingness to move from the relative security of the self to the apparent insecurity of the community. But once the move is made we realise that our freedom lies in our involvement with the community and not in our rejection of it.

However, it is one thing to take the plunge and enter in, and another to cope with what happens next. When we come to a moment like sharing the peace the theory of what should happen and what actually does happen tend to be poles apart. Unless, that is, we believe that sharing peace between people is a ritualistic gesture and nothing more. If this is the case it has no practical purpose and might just as well be cut. It has to be more than ritual if it is to involve us in the experience of sharing something together. The reason it is so often a hollow gesture is because of the fear of involvement. Psychologically it is difficult to know why we should be afraid of opening ourselves to other people, and if we try to work it out for ourselves it doesn't necessarily bring us much closer to putting it into practice. The fact is we still have to take a leap of faith and allow ourselves to be vulnerable. I've chosen, in my example of sharing the peace, perhaps the most difficult act of involvement in worship, although from my experience there are several aspects of worship that are capable of seriously upsetting people. This is because involvement touches the deepest psychological areas of our make-up. But as followers of Christ we are presumably wanting to be like him and he was intimately involved with all sorts of people. So, unless we are seriously disturbed, in which case we need professional help, we must take the plunge and involve ourselves in all stages of worship if we want to become whole people. If we don't, we are refusing to be full members of Christ's family and our celebration of his victory over the powers of selfishness becomes increasingly difficult to sustain.

It really is no good singing about love unless we try to live it. There really is no point in listening to a lesson about charity unless we try and practise it. Listening to a sermon on the resurrection will do us no good if we don't try to believe in it. Offering each other signs of peace is hollow if we don't mean it. Prayer is a nonsense if we don't long to be transformed into the likeness of God and yearn for God's love to be felt by other people. But all of these things demand involvement, a creative outlook and a willingness to change. Involvement means being creative, being willing to change, allowing the Spirit of God to come into our lives and transform us from darkness to light.

Celebration

How many services of worship have you attended where you felt glad the service had ended; where you felt you had done your duty and could forget all that had happened? Or perhaps the questions should be rephrased. How often have you felt you wanted to remain forever in the house of God? How often have you felt compelled to stay on? How often have you felt moved to celebrate your worship? If we feel nothing going on inside us as a result of worship then our worship is unconvincing and our response will be the same. If we keep coming out without experiencing some hope then it is time for us to call the Samaritans.

Worship that generates no sense of hope in the congregation is worship that is going to be playing a less important role than the Department of Social Security. It is absolutely no good having services of worship that fail to celebrate the healing power of God. This response comes from the deep desire to communicate with God in order to receive and celebrate his inestimable gift of love. Services that leave out this stage of worship eventually fizzle out. They echo the slogan found as a piece of grafitti in a London theatre, 'Due to a lack of interest tomorrow has been cancelled'. Worship becomes redundant when it has nothing to celebrate and it will only spring up again when there is a renewed call to celebrate the healing power of God. Going to church and not celebrating God's omnipotent love makes a mockery of God. It is to accept his gift of life while refusing to say thank you with a smile.

We should not be shocked by congregations dwindling and churches closing when there is no sense of celebration. When those outside the church see no visible change occurring in the lives of the people within, the conclusion must be drawn that there is nothing going on inside which is worth having. In the end all that we can speak about is the sense of celebration we see in the lives of those committed to the Christian path.

Initially our celebration of worship may start off being like the candle that is kept under the bushel, but if it stays under the bushel it will go out. It needs the air of the world for its continued existence. When it meets this world it shines for all to see. Celebration of our worship is the next step we must take in our commitment to reach out to the world. If we are to reach out to a thirsty world we must be able to offer it the water of life. Celebration in worship is the stage at which we declare the realisation that we have this water of life. If we don't celebrate this fact then we are either refusing to give thanks for the experience of God or we are not experiencing any benefits from worship. If the latter is the case we need to look very carefully at how we are approaching each of the previous stages of worship. Somewhere down the line we will be failing to allow the experience of God to come through. If the former is the case then we are not giving ourselves time to recollect that we have something to be thankful for. Celebration is the responsibility of the group. It has to be a personal tribute first of all, otherwise it merely becomes an exercise in uniformity which is unlikely to be genuine.

The mutual desire of a congregation to bless God has, first of all, to come out of a personal recognition, if it is to be real. This recognition comes when we pause to reflect on the benefits we may have received from God, for it is those benefits we shall be taking out into the world. This is the true taste of Paradise, that comes not just to the happy members of the congregation, but also to those who are bearing burdens; the people who for one reason or another are finding it impossible to be openly joyful. Paradise might only touch us in the deepest recesses of our soul, assuring us that God is with us and all will be well, but it is still enough for us to make an act of celebration. Even at our lowest it is important to be thankful, because it is in the recognition of God's goodness to us that we begin to reach Heaven.

Conclusion

I have noticed that people frequently don't know when to stop. You know, the party which begins to drag or the guests who don't know when to leave, the best man who can't resist yet another anecdote or the singer who holds the note too long. It all becomes self-indulgent. The feelings of others are forgotten. Of course God rejoices in receiving our adoration. He never ceases to tire of our outpourings of love. But God isn't interested in self-righteousness, or self-praise. We must make sure that our worship is directed towards him and not ourselves. It is not the quantity of time that we give to worship that's important, it is the quality of time that we give that matters.

It has often struck me that God is astonishingly patient with us mortals. I can only conclude that he must have an enormous sense of humour. I suppose seen from a distance many of our antics are very funny, especially when we take ourselves too seriously, but when we start to become self-indulgent the humour's gone. In the past if a performer became self-indulgent people would start to throw things at him. A hail of rotten eggs, tomatoes, orange peel and banana skins would soon bring the performance to a conclusion. The performer got off before anything worse was thrown at him. A very salutary way of being told that enough's enough. The point is, once we become self-indulgent we are no longer communing with God, we are communing with ourselves to the exclusion of God, and the sooner we conclude our reverie the better. The land of the lotus eaters is never far away from the land of reality. If the road to God is steep and narrow it is in order to keep us alert to his presence.

Once we have completed the cycle of coming to God, opening ourselves up to him, learning, understanding, responding and involving ourselves with him we need to bring our worship to a positive conclusion. This really shows the measure of our respect. If we beg audience with a king and an audience is granted and if, after the proper formalities are completed, we petition him with requests and these are also granted, we should not prolong our stay beyond the allotted time. We would be wise to express our grateful thanks and exit on cue.

The ending of a service of worship is important. It should direct us towards the future. To prolong our thanksgiving is to begin to forget the reason for being thankful. The measure of our gratitude is to be found, not in the prolongation of worship, but in the way we nurture and utilise what has been given to us.

The art of bringing worship to a conclusion needs careful consideration. Knowing when to stop is an art. Even Shakespeare sometimes outstays his welcome and we feel, like Mr Bennet in *Pride and Prejudice*, that we have been delighted long enough. But Shakespeare knew that 'good plays prove the better by the help of good epilogues'. The epilogue of a church service is generally a concluding prayer. The art of making this reflect the mood and theme of the service should not be underestimated or laid aside. It is the concise summation of what has gone before which gives us the focus for what we should be taking out, into the world.

If we have been granted God's Holy Spirit, what are we going to do with him when we leave the church? That is the question to which we should either already know the answer, or be storing up for future consideration and prayer. If we have received this gift and don't use it it will be taken away from us. We must leave with the intention of sharing our gifts with a hungry world. Then we will ourselves be nourished by it, and when we return for more, more will be given to us. If we are uncertain as to what to do we need only ask God to show us the way. The way will quickly become obvious when we start to reach out to the world. Reaching out to the world is the final stage of worship which comes from the very heart of the church. We are the vessels that carry its gift of salvation to all the people we meet as we move through life. The art of being the servants of God is a creative act that knows no end, just as God's creativity knows no end.

Stewardship

If you make the decision to go on holiday to the place of your dreams and you decide to go there under your own steam, and not as part of a package holiday, you have to make careful plans in order to get there. Good organisation is something most of us try to avoid unless we are bound to it by the necessity of our own work. But without it the layout of the holiday, or the layout of worship, has no structure. It becomes spineless and flabby and there is nothing exciting or invigorating about it. Good stewardship provides us with a layout which will get us to our destination.

But good organisation should not be tactless supervision. That is bad stewardship. Obtrusive organisation merely distracts our attention. It is over-concerned with its own importance. It prevents us from being able to explore the spiritual realm to any depth because it is always dragging us back to the surface of things. It occurs when the administration of worship has become more important than the purpose for which the worship was designed. It takes over completely when the purpose of worship is lost and becomes the blind hand of authority leading the blinkered vision of its adherents. This is when we start to hear phrases like: 'Our services of worship are in a rut', 'What does it all mean?', 'What are we doing here?', 'Why aren't there more people in the church?'

The balance between good stewardship and the celebration of worship is a delicate one. One of the problems that occurs in the world of the theatre is that the balance between the stewardship of the theatre and its artistic life is upset. Sometimes you notice in theatre programmes that the administrative staff far outweigh the number of people appearing on the stage. If savings have to be made, in order to keep the theatre running, then the cry goes out that it is the size of the cast which must be cut. Rarely is the number of administrators running the establishment cut back. But without the product stewardship ceases to have any validity, even though the product is dependent on the stewardship.

A balance has to be struck and it is in maintaining this balance that good stewardship becomes an art in itself. Great art is very good at disguising itself. The greatness has to be sought out because it is presented in such a simple way that we can easily miss its genius. Look at the creative genius of God and how easily we take that for granted. That is how good stewardship should be. It should be the unseen servant of the spirit of worship. It should be a willing and pliable steward, ready to wait, ready to step in, ready to change direction at the slightest command. If one's stewardship is incapable of being malleable it will either break under the strain of the creative power of worship or it will suffocate the creative spirit in its rigidity. Then the experience will be like a soap opera, titillating for a time but quickly reducing our reactions to a level of extreme banality. When we go to services where we are told what to say, what to think, what to do and when to do things, without being given time to reflect, or to act for ourselves, then it is obvious that the stewardship of the service has become dictatorial. It has taken over to the detriment of the creativity of worship. There ceases to be any malleability for the Spirit of God to shine through.

On the other hand when we go to services where emotions are whipped up to the point where our ability to reason clearly is swamped by emotionalism, then it is obvious that the stewardship has abdicated its God-given responsibility to give people the freedom to make their own decisions. In neither situation is there a sense of artistic or creative balance. There is either a dogmatic straight-jacket or an emotional manipulation, which, in the hands of the unscrupulous, produces awful results.

True artistry is concerned with revealing the truth. It shuns stereotyped emotion and prototyped thought. It seeks the delicate balance which allows us to produce the right equation for creative worship. So the artistic handling of God's ministry is important, both for the purpose of the service, and for the ongoing life that the service engenders.

If we have a balanced stewardship that allows the Spirit of God to shine through then the outcome of that worship will be the desire to carry God's Spirit into the world. This is the natural consequence of creative worship that is kept in balance with good stewardship. But the responsibility for good stewardship does not stop at the end of a service. Good stewardship of worship is the learning ground for our behaviour and outreach into the world at large.

Outreach

If having concluded our worship we return to the world without having changed, even one iota, then something is either seriously wrong with our worship or we believe that worship should have no bearing on what we do in the world. If the first is the case then we need to pinpoint the problems and put them right. But if we believe that worship shouldn't involve us in having to change ourselves then we need to beware. Worship is not a static affair. We either grow through worship or we shrink. If worship is meaningless or dull then our interest in worship will wither away. But if it is fulfilling we become people filled with the Spirit of God. This passion for God cannot remain in a vacuum. It either draws the world into its midst or it bursts out onto the world. A lit candle cannot remain under a bushel. It will either suffocate or burn its way out. The privileged gift we have been given in worship has to be shared if it is to survive. We have to take our experience of worship into the world, and if worship is as enriching as it ought to be, then it becomes imperative for us to witness to God and to become stewards of his world. So within our worship we need to bear in mind the fact that we are heralds and stewards of God's Kingdom.

Sometimes it is felt that the role of proclamation is the

only task that Christians need to undertake. But proclamation without action is worthless. We have to act out what we believe, or we become like the Priest and the Levite who passed by on the other side in the story of the Good Samaritan. It's useless our proclaiming the good news to the world if our actions in the world do not live up to what we are proclaiming. It is important to tell people that through belief in Christ we are saved from our sins and brought into partnership with God because it is true, but that is not the whole story. God sent Jesus, not only to save us from death, but also to provide us with the way to live our lives in conjunction with God and our fellow human beings. The Gospels of Matthew, Mark, Luke and John give us a very clear picture of how we are to go about this task in a truly creative way.

So part of our worship needs to train us for Christian behaviour and action if we are to have any effect on the world. It has to be a form of training which stretches us week by week, or service by service. For example, as I mentioned in the section on involvement, it has become fairly common within part of Christian worship to offer each other the sign of peace. Unfortunately this often becomes a ritualistic action demanding the minimum effort from its practitioners. Some people say it is an unnecessary gesture and others don't want, or won't have, anything to do with it. But this gesture of peace is the outward sign of our Christian attitude and proclamation to the world. 'By this shall all people know that you are my disciples, if you have love one to another' (John 13:35). It is difficult, if not impossible, to love someone openly without displaying some outward sign of that love. We need to test our faith with actions within our worship because if we find it difficult to practise them there, we will certainly find it impossible to practise them outside. We are called to be like Christ and in order for us to do this we must focus our attention on Christ's behaviour and learn to practise this behaviour in our worship in order that we may practise it in our lives. We are called to be stewards of

God's world and so we must first of all learn what that means, practically, within the church.

3

Creative Questions

There are three questions which are essential to the process of creative action and they are the questions what, why, and how. The questions that all artists have to ask themselves every time they start a new piece of work are: 'What am I doing?', 'Why am I doing it?' and 'How am I going to achieve it?' If you think about it these are the questions everyone has to ask themselves every day of their lives. But most of the time these questions are not being asked on a conscious level. If they were we would be stopping and starting all the time. This questioning process becomes habitual and subconscious. But often this internal process is not able to function as it should. The reason for this is that people rarely allow themselves long enough to digest information adequately, before responding. Consequently they make hurried decisions that naturally lead to mistakes. Everyone will be well aware of these occasions in their lives. But on a deeper level the situation becomes more chronic. The more we rush our creative decision making processes, the more we squeeze our creative faculties, which need space. They need time and tranquillity to function at their best. If we refuse them these things they cease to operate.

Our society sets great store by the phrase 'Time is Money'. But though it has set a price on time it has not recognised its value. If getting and spending, in as short a time as possible is the dominant obsession then it is not surprising that most people's creative faculties appear to be virtually non-existent. Children up to the age of nine or ten are allowed to waste time but once the rush for scholastic results is on, then creativity begins to take a back seat. It requires quite an effort and a considerable nerve to stand against the pressures of modern progress. Time is at a premium and yet it is time that we have, first of all, got to learn to waste. Until we dare to waste time our creative faculties don't stand a chance because they are given no space to work in their own way.

Unfortunately this means having to wait, not just for quarter of an hour but for as long as it takes for the subconscious to produce the answer. We have been schooled to think that our intellectual faculties can produce the right answers automatically. The creative faculties are far more mysterious than that. They are not dependent on intellect. They work on their own and produce answers in their own time. Unless we are prepared to trust their mysterious skill they produce nothing. The creative process is a power that operates so deep within us that it is never completely accessible to our conscious minds. We are calling upon the creative energy that controls the world. That energy comes from God and we can feel God to be at work in us if we give ourselves time. So time is a vital ingredient in the process of our asking the creative questions that will liberate creative answers. It was only after weeks of research that Kekule's dream gave him the answer to the molecular structure of Benzine. 'What is this life if, full of care, we have no time to stand and stare', wrote the poet W. H. Davies.

I remember seeing my father spend hours just looking out of the windows of our house. I could not begin to guess what he was thinking or whether, in the accepted sense of that word, he was thinking at all. I doubt if he could have told me himself. The gaze was still and contemplative, fixed but not rigid. What I do know is that these periods of contemplation were always followed by creative action. Either he would redesign a part of the garden, or he would begin to paint a new picture. This process came to him quite naturally. I don't think it was always comfortable, but the waiting for him was an essential part of the creation.

The soufflé is the most delicate of dishes but opening the

oven door to see how it is getting on will almost guarantee its failure to rise. Our creativity is like that soufflé: it needs time and a certain amount of privacy to develop. It requires patience and a good deal of faith before we see significant results. We have to be willing and sometimes rather uncomprehending partners in this mysterious process.

But are we prepared to give way in such an absolute manner? If we are not then the creative impulse and its results will diminish. Perhaps we don't care much about creativity and feel that it is not an essential ingredient in our worship. But our birth was a creative act, every decision, every move in our lives has its creative aspect. God's creativity is always at work in us and our duty is to align ourselves completely with it. The astonishing fact is that God is asking not merely for our consent, or acceptance of his will, but for our collaboration in his purposes. He longs for our creative companionship, but he never forces us to labour for him.

To deny creativity is to deny God's love. It is to deny life itself. The consequences are boredom, sterility, frustration, anger and illness. It produces that numbing sense of futility which we see around us in so much of our contemporary life. When we cease to ask ourselves the answers to the questions, 'What am I doing?' and 'Why am I doing it?', we are condemning ourselves to a monotonous existence. Once we know what we want to do and why we want to do it we are on the way to becoming fully alive.

Pray, meditate, contemplate. If we have no time for these then we have no time for God. To watch God's creative process in the world around us is to respond to the creative process that is alive in each one of us. That creativity is a sleeping giant which, when awakened, can change the world.

As Christians we are not searching in a void nor are we unaware of the subject matter that we wish to work on. We already have our subject matter to hand. We are starting with a distinct advantage because we have already asked these questions and they have brought us the knowledge that it is through

Christ we will find the answers and it is in the church we will find Christ. We have discovered that it is in our services of worship that the church offers us that means of reaching God through Christ. The situation we have now reached is that of asking more specific and searching questions about the nature of our worship in order to deepen it and make it come more fully alive.

The Question 'What?'

When two people fall in love they have no difficulty in worshipping the ground each other stands on but after the honeymoon period there comes a time when they have to start working at their relationship. This is when they begin to question what it is all about. It is not a question of being dissatisfied or disillusioned, though that might be the case. It is a question of needing to know how it all works. It becomes important to re-ask the questions, 'What am I doing? What is going on?', not in order to get out but in order to fulfil the purpose which has brought them together.

Unfortunately these questions are often not answered because we are frightened of hearing the answers. But what are we frightened of? If we are frightened of hearing the truth then we are coming to the wrong place anyway. The church is the haven where we can find the truth. It isn't an earthly court of law that will condemn us to life imprisonment. It is the heavenly court which provides the law of love that leads to freedom.

What is there to be frightened of if we ask the questions that lead us towards the truth? I suspect that we are not frightened of freedom, we all want that, we are frightened of what it might entail. Work. Work on ourselves. The work that involves us in a transformation: a personal revolution.

There is nothing more painful than having to do something about our reluctance to change. This is not, as some think, a process which happens only once, at the moment of our conversion to Christianity. It is an ongoing process because following Christ involves us in a creative transformation which lasts for a lifetime. To follow means to obey, and to obey means being continually prepared to break new ground, in our desire to become more like the person of Christ. It is a challenge that wills us to ask the questions that lead to the answers. The answers involve change and we know that. That is why we can be so unwilling to ask the questions in the first place. We always hope that we can stay where we are, and as we are, but that is impossible. We can either grow creatively towards the likeness of Christ or we can shrink into the inactivity of death. If we want to grow in our worship we must be creative in asking the questions that lead to fresh insight and renewed vigour.

My experience of working with church groups has led to the conclusion that very few people have a clear understanding of what is going on. To ask such simple questions as, 'What is the liturgy about?', 'What are the readings for?', may seem childish and obvious but once these questions are asked we may be surprised by how little we know.

But the question 'what' on its own can only reveal a static answer of truth. 'What is singing for?' may produce the answer, 'It is for praising God' or 'It is for our edification' or 'It is a way of helping us to learn about God'. Yet the answers do not in themselves result in any form of action. If we ask this question on its own and don't back it up with further questions we are in danger of being content with superficial knowledge alone. We would be contenting ourselves with half-truths and selling ourselves short. We would not be immersing ourselves in the whole truth which involves knowing the answers through practical experiences.

This unwillingness to go the whole way is a common problem. In his encounters with people Jesus was never content with simple panaceas, he penetrated to the roots of the problem. In the case of the rich young man the questions that Jesus asked and the solutions that he gave were too penetrating.

Before we go on let us summarise the things that are to be achieved from asking the question 'what'.

First of all it is the leading creative question, the question that small children persistently ask their parents, 'Mummy, Daddy, what is this?' 'What does it do?', the question we should be totally unafraid of asking our heavenly Father. Secondly, although it appears to be a simple question and we think we already know the answers it almost always reveals a host of responses we had never considered before. Thirdly, we need courage to ask it, knowing that it cannot do us, or anyone else, any harm if it is asked in good faith. Fourthly, it is a question that needs to go on being asked at different stages of our development because it always has the capability of leading us towards greater spiritual understanding. Finally, it is a question that can be asked in an endless variety of ways.

That makes it a far more interesting question than any to be found in Trivial Pursuit!

The Question 'Why?'

The question 'why?' goes deeper. It probes the foundations of those answers produced by the question 'what?' It brings us face to face with our own inadequate knowledge and experience of the depth of things. It is the kind of question we spend all of our time running away from. 'Mummy, what is a star?' 'A star, darling, is something that shines in the sky. Look, there's a star up there.' 'What's it doing up there?' 'It's shining in the sky, darling.' 'Why's it shining in the sky, Mummy?' And suddenly we are floored by the depth of the question. We find it relatively easy to answer the 'what' type of questions because, on the whole, our education has equipped us with an understanding of the surface of things and it is fairly easy for us to provide a whole series of answers on this level. If the child had persisted with 'What's it doing shining in the sky, Mummy?', we could answer, 'Because it's giving us its light'. But if the question came back, 'Why is it giving us its light?', we find we are being drawn into a mysterious, unknown realm. We choose to leave this sort of question to the scientist or the theologian but we would be wise to try and tackle it for ourselves.

There are at least five ways of approaching this mystery: we can ignore it. We can refuse to answer, or tell the child to shut up. We can refuse to question it, responding, 'Because that's the way it is'. We can provide materialistic answers, which use science as their basis of revelation. There is the mystical answer which relies on poetic imagination; story-telling. And then there is the answer that acknowledges, alongside the child, that here indeed is a great wonder that deserves to be contemplated. This last approach leads towards our building a philosophical and theological framework. And this in turn gives us an answer that is composed partly of poetic imagination and partly of scientific facts. We construct an understanding for ourselves that uses all the knowledge we have at our command and which is fleshed out with experiences that corroborate and give life to our knowledge. The problems arise when we believe that our knowledge is complete, without error, and it is then that we are often caught out by the question 'why'. It takes a great deal of humility to face this kind of questioning. If, like the child, we have the courage to be completely honest, we discover the freedom to be found in admitting we do not know the answers to some of the most basic questions about our worship. This leads to a far deeper appreciation of the mystery. But we tend to be frightened of mystery because it means we are not in control.

The problem is that we are afraid of the question 'why' because it uncovers what lies beneath. It will expose the depths of our ignorance and shatter our hard won emotional stability. But, like bicycle riders, we maintain our balance by moving forward. We must grow or wither. Religious experience involves exploration. It takes us into the hidden areas of our life that are usually only revealed to us in dreams. Religious experience only becomes possible when we cease to be frightened of asking the question 'why'.

The question 'why' is the beginning of our descent into the centre of ourselves, where we discover what makes us believe in the things we have taken for granted. The question 'why' is, to begin with, uncomfortable. If we find this unacceptable then we have not yet come to terms with the nature of salvation, which heals with the surgeon's knife. If we have no desire to know then what are we doing in the church anyway? If we think we already know then what is wrong with having another look?

If we refuse to look it almost certainly means that we are not sure of the answers, in which case it is foolish not to find out. The blind leading the blind end up in the ditch.

One of the problems Jesus had with his disciples was not that they kept on asking him awkward questions but that they thought they already knew the answers. They all got it wrong and Jesus had to warn them that their belief was shallow. If Peter had kept on asking Jesus the question, 'Why are you like this?', he might not have lost so much faith in Jesus at the time of his trial and crucifixion. It was only after Jesus' death that the disciples started to ask why it had all happened the way it did. When the answer came to them at Pentecost they were ready to set the world on fire with the truth of the Gospel.

'Why?' is an uncomfortable question that unnerves parents of small children but doesn't worry God in the least. On the contrary it delights God to be taken so seriously. It is the point from which he can begin to reveal his glory to those who ask. When we start asking the question in relation to our services of worship the answers can be startling. But they will remain unsatisfactory until we start to put them into practice with the final creative question 'How?'

The Question 'How?'

The question 'how' is the most daunting of the three because it demands that we bridge the gap between the world of speculative thought and the world of action. It provides us with the uncomfortable challenge of seeing whether we can transfer what we think we can do into a reality. It will indeed be the most difficult question of the three to answer, in fact it will be impossible to answer if we haven't spent sufficient time on the first two questions. If those initial questions have been thoroughly explored then we stand a much better chance of being able to tackle the question 'how' successfully. Why? Because we shall have spent time getting our imaginations to work. The question 'why', if asked intelligently, begins to take us past the barriers of logical, materialistic, scientific thought, towards the realm of imaginative and poetic thought. Here the answers are more elusive. We find them harder to formulate.

The question 'how' demands action. Action is something most of us want to avoid. Speculation is one thing, turning it into action is quite another. We tend not to like trying new things because of the possibility of failure. One of the things human beings hate being faced with is the knowledge that they are not in control. It's all right to say, 'I can't do something therefore I won't'. That leaves the truth of whether you could do it, if you tried, mercifully hidden. But if you are surrounded by people who tell you, 'You can do it', then your reluctance is seen for what it is: laziness and fear. You are faced with the fact that it is your reticence to move, and fear of failure, that makes you say, 'I can't, therefore I won't'.

Once one accepts the fact that it takes time to accomplish anything worth while, that in the early stages the results will look pretty ludicrous and may be minimal, one is half-way to achieving the result. But there is another barrier which can be an even greater stumbling block to having a go, and that is the belief that one has got to be able to achieve a professional's standards. In order to sing a solo one has got to sing like

Placido Domingo; in order to paint a landscape one has to be able to paint like Constable; in order to play the piano one has got to be able to play like Rachmaninov.

If a person is thinking of performing in public then these criteria might well apply but it is quite the wrong standpoint to take when it comes to looking into the possibilities of revitalising worship. It is not my intention to encourage Christians to become performers in the field of the arts, but if we involve ourselves in creative activity, the creative arts can help us to appreciate that worship is a complete experience; an experience that encompasses body, mind and spirit. There is no doubt that involvement in an artistic activity makes it far easier to provide answers to the question, 'What can we do about the state of our worship?' It isn't possible for the intellectual faculty to work it all out because worship is an activity where we enter the realms of poetic and imaginative truth and our worship is only fulfilled through being involved with poetic and imaginative answers. These answers are not dependent on our skill as artists but on our commitment to the creative approach. Practice is the key to our success. It was Blake who said, 'If the fool will persist in his folly he will becomes wise.'

What we need to know is how we can make our services of worship become the most vital part of our existence. The answer is through experimentation in the arts and an artistic approach should be the framework for every service. When we know this is so we realise that by asking the question 'how', and acting upon it, we have begun to tread a path of pure joy that leads us straight to the heart of God. It helps us come together as a creative worshipping community and it helps us to construct a vision of living Paradise.

4

Creative Answers

In chapter 2 I tended to concentrate on some of the negative aspects of what can be found in the various stages of worship. The point that needed to be made was that the negative side of worship frequently confronts people when they participate in a service. The purpose was not to denigrate the good things that are happening but to be critical and honest about the non-productive areas. The purpose of criticism is not to do harm, or poke fun but to highlight those areas that are in need of constructive attention. In painting a general picture the aim has been to produce a positive reaction of, 'Yes, our services of worship, or parts of them, are very similar to the pictures that have been drawn in these chapters.' If this is in any way the case then it is important for us to be humble enough to admit these truths and concerned enough to be determined to put them right. If we don't put them right we only have our-selves to blame when we become ineffective voices to a world that is longing for spiritual truth and comfort and we become responsible for such laziness.

We have heard Christ himself say: 'Let your light so shine before men that they may see your good works and glorify your father which is in heaven' (Matt. 5:16). We are told not to be like the person who hides their candle under a bushel or buries their talent in the ground. We have been told that if we have seen the light we must share it.

How can it be done?

In Luke's Gospel Jesus suggests that we should, 'Ask, seek and knock' (11:9). When we keep on asking we finally get answers to our questions. When we keep on seeking we find what we are looking for. When we keep on knocking the door is eventually opened for us. The process can take a long time because we have to be accurate in the questions we ask, and we have to ask the questions in the right way. It's no good stopping in the centre of a busy city, hailing the nearest passer-by, and expecting him to be able to tell us how we find our way to the house of a friend of ours who we think may live in the north, or perhaps the south, or could it be the east, or west of the city, and to expect an answer that will be of much use to us. Someone asked the writer Gertrude Stein on her death-bed 'What is the answer?' to which she very sensibly replied, 'What is the question?' So the first step that we have to take is to ask the right questions and to be prepared to take time finding out what they are.

When we start asking questions we may feel as though we are in dense fog or even total darkness. It takes time to understand and cope with what is going on inside. The initial stages of creativity are subterranean and unintelligible. It is like groping around in the middle of the night for the light switch. We need to experiment, to explore, to feel our way towards a recognisable answer. All we may be aware of to start with is a yearning for clarity, for light. It is a thoroughly uncomfortable feeling and we probably want to shy away from it, but we mustn't. It is the inspiration of God's Spirit at work in us. He is calling us to search for him and we will remain unsatisfied until we have discovered where he is leading us. If we persist in asking creative questions it may take time for the truth to emerge but when it does everything inside us responds. It is as though a spark has set off a train of reactions that suddenly make us sure we are on the right path and we become impatient to start searching. But it is difficult to be certain that we are right. If we have a friend, a member of our family, someone in the church or a spiritual director who can help us we will be well advised to seek their help. Sometimes we need the advice of someone else to assure us that we are not barking up the wrong tree. It is important, when we set out on a spiritual journey, to make sure we are travelling in the right direction and searching for the right clues. So how do we start?

We start in silence. If we are working together in a group it is important to have someone guiding the discussion. If we are on our own we need to set ourselves apart from our everyday world in order to find creative answers to our search for fulfilled and inspiring worship.

Take a journey away from this noisy world of ours for a while. Find a place where you can be alone. It can be a room in your house, the garden, a park, somewhere in the country-side, a retreat house, anywhere where you will be undisturbed. A place where you can be at peace and look at your worship in a state of meditation. Let yourself rest in God for a while until your spirit is at peace. Then refreshed and at ease let your mind range over the whole experience of your worship until it settles on the area that is troubling you. Then start to ask the creative questions and go on asking them until you have pinpointed the things that are wrong with your worship.

But creative change in the approach to our worship is not always met with an open-hearted welcome.

Let us take the most depressing scenario we can find. Our church is old, cold, dark and dank. The arrangement of the church makes it impossible for worship to have any malleability whatsoever. The Sunday service is antiquated. The congregation are apathetic. The priest, the church wardens and church elders are bastions of conservatism and will not even contemplate the idea of any changes taking place. There is no other church that we can decamp to and anyway we want to stay where we live. What on earth can we do about it?

Admittedly the cards are stacked against us and there doesn't appear to be much we can do to alter the situation. But we do have a choice. We can do nothing, in which case we shall continue to smoulder, which will be no good for anyone. Or, we can cast around for some improvements. Let's concentrate on just one of the problems.

There are so many things wrong with this particular church that it is hard to know where to focus our attention first. Of course the biggest problem we've got is the intractability of the people in charge of the church. Does this mean that we should subjugate ourselves to their way of doing things? If we do we will continue to be unhappy and it will show through in unhelpful ways. On the other hand if we start being critical of the present state of affairs we will certainly arouse a great deal of animosity. Is this the only way of trying to effect change? Perhaps we should make sure first of all, with someone we can trust, that our cause for unrest is valid. If it is then it is important for us to take a planned course of action. Can we do this in a Christian manner? It is true that a good discussion, even a heated argument, can produce healthy results but would it work in this situation?

Yes, this may well be the first move but from experience we know a discussion is unlikely to produce results. We've tried to talk about possible alterations to the church and different ways of approaching our worship and we've met with very definite resistance. If we allow a discussion to evolve into an argument we can be pretty certain that we will have shut the door against change for a very long time. Therefore confrontation is not the way, in this instance, to effect change. We need to start at a point where we will meet with the least resistance and work from there. After all, if we succeed in proving that a little change results in increased awareness and enjoyment, we will be that much closer to being able to effect greater change. Where can we start?

Whatever we do we have to start with the acceptance of the leader of the church. There is always something that they will be happy for us to do. It may be as mundane as cleaning the church which can lead to suggesting that some of the rubbish at the back is removed. If the church is made spotlessly clean then it will become even more evident that the place needs repainting. Are there a group of people who could be inveigled into doing it? Perhaps it could start with repainting the vestry or the entrance hall? In the end it is our energy, enthusiasm, commitment and sensitivity to the feelings of others that will set the creative momentum going and encourage people to join in our efforts. However we shouldn't expect the task to be easy or quick in achieving results. We need the patience and the perseverance of a saint if we are to achieve a creative atmosphere of worship amidst difficult surroundings.

There is no point in trying to run before we can walk. If we find that we are in a church which appears to be antagonistic to change of any sort we must move slowly, carefully and thoughtfully. We must be prepared for only minor and seemingly insignificant advances. They may appear to have no bearing on creative worship but they are in fact the foundation stones for an atmosphere of openness and growth which, later on, will allow miracles of creativity in worship to occur.

Human beings, says Plato, are like people in a cave lit by fire. They watch shadows dancing on the wall cast by the fire. Then they turn round and see the fire, and the wooden puppets that are casting the shadows. So they venture outside into the sunlight. At first the light is too dazzling for them to look into the sun; they have to look at the objects on which the sun shines. Then they look at the sun's reflection in the water, then at the sun itself, the source of all light. But, continues Plato, once they are able to do this, they must venture back into the cave to lead others to the light. And the cave will seem a very dark and shadowy place indeed to those who have seen the true light.

People who have realised that communal worship needs to be creative, if it is to survive, are like the human beings who have dared to venture out of the cave and look at their worship in the light of God's creativity. It provides an intoxicating vision of how things can be. But just as the light at first dazzled those coming out of Plato's cave, so the vision of creative worship will dazzle those still incarcerated in moribund worship. Don't force this vision on people, it will only blind them to change. Effect change slowly so that people can get used to the fact that it makes their worship more alive and vibrant. Be subtle and sensitive and win people round to your vision. Then when you have got everyone behind you you can begin to venture into using the creative arts to help revitalise the whole of your worship.

Notes

1. Keep on asking the right questions.
2. Don't give up.
3. Find somewhere peaceful to think.
4. Always start in silence, whether in a group or on one's own.
5. Use a good friend as a sounding board.
6. Work from a position of acceptance.
7. Start by finding the areas people are happy to have changed.
8. Keep a low profile, if necessary, like yeast in the dough.
9. Be prepared to go it alone.
10. Don't run before you can walk.
11. Effect change slowly.
12. Don't force your vision on other people, be subtle.
13. Always be sensitive and considerate to others.
14. Don't let frustration supersede the virtues of patience and love.
15. Maintain the patience of a saint.

The following episodes contain twelve illustrated stories, all completely fictitious but drawn from my experience of taking workshops in churches of all denominations and persuasions. They illustrate how, once we have reached a position where the mood of the church is favourable, we can begin to effect creative workshops which are designed to enrich our understanding and appreciation of worship. Each episode has its parallel episode in the chapter on 'Stages of Worship', in order to show how a creative attitude can change the attitude of each stage of worship.

Every episode involves a different church and different people, but all the situations could be found in any place. They are not unusual. They show how a natural pattern of creativity evolves for each person and how, if we want to, we can set up creative workshops that can follow quite natural patterns.

If I were to lay out specific workshops for people to follow I would be doing them a great disservice. I would be blocking the progress of individual patterns of creativity. The only way of avoiding this problem is to provide readers with a sort of parable. Then, with the help provided in the chapter on 'Creative Questions', and in the examples given in chapters 5, 6 and 7, the reader's creative instincts and imagination can do the rest.

A General Layout for Creative Workshops

1. Start off with a time of apparent inactivity to allow the body, mind and spirit time to rest in a state of meditation and contemplation.
2. Work out the answers to the questions: 'What do we want to do?', 'Why do we want to do it?', 'How are we going to achieve a result?'
3. Formulate a plan of action.
4. Give yourselves plenty of time to bring the idea to birth.
5. Take a break.
6. Fashion the idea into a recognisable shape.
7. Stand back and enjoy what you have done.
8. Reflect on what you have learnt.
9. Put into action what you have learnt.

Episode One: Inspiration

It was six o'clock on a Sunday morning. Peter, a man in his late forties, had been unable to sleep properly all night. He had decided to get up and make himself a cup of tea. He had put on a dressing gown and shuffled down to the kitchen which was bathed in the icy gold of early morning sunshine. The tea made, he had plumped himself down by the window looking out onto the garden. Everything was still and silent. The grass glittered with beads of dew. Everything should have been lovely, but it wasn't. Peter felt that there was no longer any point to his existence.

Peter worked in insurance and commuted every day into London from the suburbs. He was married with two children, but was not happy. His marriage was mundane, his work tedious and his church was uninspiring. What had happened to his life? He used to find it such fun when he was young. He would argue spiritedly with friends on art, religion, politics, anything, sometimes seriously, sometimes for the sheer fun of it. He used to enjoy listening to jazz and going down to the pub and writing poetry. Nowadays his life was composed of getting to work on time, fighting to keep his job in order to pay for the mortgage and feed his family. His church life which had once been such a revelation to him had imperceptibly turned into another routine. The joy in it had gone.

He knew that he wasn't alone in this respect. There were others in his church for whom churchgoing was an ordeal rather than a delight. He used to look forward to Sundays because of the service, but no longer.

Peter's thoughts had been dwelling on this subject for some time without his having come to any definite conclusion, or taking any action. And now it was Sunday again. He had had a particularly tiring and repetitive week. He wondered whether he shouldn't stay at home after all and rest. He began doodling with a pencil on a piece of paper.

At that moment sitting in silence and writing, 'What am I doing with my life?', seemed more important to him than going to church. Here there need be no pretending that all was well when it wasn't.

'What do I want to do with my life?', he wrote. 'What am I doing? What do I want?' He paused and wrote the last two words again. 'I want . . . I want to be inspired again. I want to feel alive. I want to know why I've lost my zest for life. What can the church do about it? Or perhaps I should ask what I expect from the church. Inspiration? Yes. Why did I once feel that the church provided me with inspiration? Why did I find it so exciting? Was it because I experienced a sense of God there?'

Peter found himself writing down the question again, 'What do I want to do?', and answering it with, 'I want to worship God again'. He wrote down the question 'Why?' and followed it with the answer, 'In order to experience God again.' A sense of God . . . He had almost forgotten what that meant. He underlined the phrases, and before he knew what was happening he'd begun to write his first poem for something like twenty years.

> The road across the hill was empty,
> It was dark and almost winter,
> Lights from the valley farm flickered,
> A solitary bell's sound
> Reached up into the hills.
> It was a silent place
> Except for the owl's hoot . . .
> Voices singing filled the air . . .

Time slipped by unnoticed until he found himself writing the final lines:

> Loving from the great abundance,
> Loving things that never last.

When he had finished he found that it was seven o'clock. Half an hour had passed without his noticing it. The teapot was cold. He began to read what he had written with great care. Though he was aware already of many faults he was amazed by what he had achieved. He decided to make another pot of tea before trying to improve it.

It was the best cup of tea he'd tasted in ages. When he'd finished it he set about discarding all the things that seemed irrelevant and concentrated his efforts on shaping the poem effectively. Another half an hour passed by which time he felt he had done all he could to get it right.

Looking at the final result he realised that he had truly achieved something. He put on the kettle for yet another cup of tea and gave his arms and legs a good stretch. A renewed sense of life was coursing through him. Perhaps a renewed sense of God? What had happened? He looked at the final result.

A Sense of God

> Simple silence, quiet peace,
> Concentration stretched in time,
> Endless waiting for a coming
> Never made but always there
> Fragrant blossoms lifting senses
> Into regions long forlorn,
> Waiting, waiting like a servant
> For his presence to appear
> Silence bringing wells of stillness,
> Eyes enclosed within a shell,
> Beauty stretching out a handshake
> Handshakes turning to a kiss,
> Embraces of a free endeavour,
> Loving from a great abyss.

It might not be perfect but it would do. Reading it again he understood that, quite without meaning to, he'd written down all the things that had been missing in his life for so long. They were things that he could ill afford to do without, and yet they had been shoved aside by his present hectic and unconvincing lifestyle.

Simplicity, silence, peace, time to concentrate undisturbed, time to wait in a suspended, eternal moment, the need for all these things seemed so clear now. Beauty could only come back into his life out of silence and the clean empty space of contemplation. This was the loving message that had come to him out of the great abyss of God. He would put his poem into action and return these things to the centre of his life.

It was time for church and he was suddenly looking forward to being there once more. He felt inspired again to worship and to reach out to others who might benefit from a similar injection of inspiration.

A poetry workshop group could be the greatest fun and could make the search for God a vivid and profound activity. Who knew where it might lead?

Notes

1. Peter was caught by the beauty of looking at his garden in the early morning. Something about its serenity and stillness allowed his whole being to relax and contemplate the situation.

2. He answered the questions, 'What do I want to do?', 'Why do I want to do it?' and 'How do I go about achieving it?' quite naturally. In a workshop the answers to these questions need to be demanded quite tenaciously if progress is to be made.

3. Peter didn't need to formulate a plan. It happened for him. But the plan of action he unconsciously followed, though not the only one, is good for a workshop such as this.

4. He spent at least half an hour letting the poem evolve in his head.

5. He gave himself a rest after this piece of work. God rested on the seventh day. A woman after giving birth needs rest. Without a break we can squeeze ourselves dry.

6. It's important to enjoy what you have done, even though you are aware of the faults. Brilliance is not our primary aim. We are trying to increase our knowledge and experience from practising our art.

7. So give yourself time to reflect on what you've done.

8. It is also important to invest what you have learnt into the

rest of your life. Share the benefit with others. If we don't do this, half the joy is lost.

Episode Two: Searching

Joan lived in a bungalow in the residential area of a small town. She was a widow in her sixties with grown-up children who had left home. She had come to live in this particular area shortly after her husband had died. The idea was for her to be near one of her married daughters. However, not long after she had settled in, her daughter and son-in-law had to go overseas for three years. For almost the first time in her life Joan found herself alone in unfamiliar surroundings with few friends and time on her hands.

It was a lonely time for her and she had taken to wandering around the neighbourhood with a sketchbook and pencil, engaging in a hobby for which previously she had had no time. She found herself spending a lot of time in churchyards. To begin with, she couldn't understand her reasons for wanting to sketch church buildings, but, having covered the immediate vicinity, it began to occur to her that she was looking for something which she had neglected most of her life.

Then she found herself returning again and again to sketch the inside of a church not far from where she lived. The place fascinated her in so many ways. She made numerous sketches from different angles in varying lights. But she discovered that it wasn't only the architecture of the church that caught her attention. There was an indefinable quality to the place which eluded her pencil and yet kept on inviting her to capture it.

During the ensuing days she began to turn the sketches she had made into full-blown water colours, and it was not long before she had completed a whole series of paintings on various aspects of the church. It was at the point when she had nearly completed the series that she found she suddenly needed to revisit the church early one Sunday morning to remind herself of the light in the church at that time of day.

It wasn't until she walked through the door that she realised she had caught the Sunday morning service. Curious but undaunted she entered in and immediately realised that she had come home at last. That indefinable quality which she had been trying vainly to capture on paper was something, she realised, that would go on eluding her. But equally, she knew, she would go on pursuing it.

It was not long before she had made many new friends in the congregation. But something surprised her very much. As she got to know the people she discovered that quite a few of them weren't happy with the church. They complained of its ugliness and inaccessibility. Joan was amazed. The place was not perfect, but it was unique and had an atmosphere all of its own. How could she help people see the beauty of what they had got?

She decided that she'd try showing people some of the paintings she'd done of the church. Perhaps they might see through her eyes some of what she had seen. The reaction to her paintings was so favourable that she was asked to mount an exhibition of them. There she was asked to explain how she'd come to do them. The enthusiastic response to her talk led to a small group within the church forming themselves into a sketching club under Joan's guidance.

Some of the dissatisfied members of the church were in the group. Joan decided to start them off with a time of quiet reflection during which they moved about the church slowly, looking at it from all angles, but making no comments about it. Then she gathered them together for a discussion which she started with the question: 'What do you want?'

All sorts of answers emerged but the one Joan chose for them to concentrate on was, 'I want to find a place for worship'. It was the answer Joan had been looking for. She believed it would lead them to rediscover what they had lost, but what was there in front of their eyes. Then she asked the question: 'Why do we want to find a place for worship?'

The simplest and most direct answer was, 'in order to meet with God'. Joan understood that answer well. It had been her unspoken desire when she had found this church. She then asked members of the group how they thought they might achieve this. In Joan's mind the answer was very simple. She had met with God through painting and sketching the church. For the group the answer was not so immediately apparent and much time was spent discussing possible answers.

Then Joan suggested that they might find the answer by sketching some favourite aspect of the church. They agreed to meet in the church hall for coffee an hour later and share the results of their work together to see how close they had individually come to an answer. Time passed quickly and pleasantly.

Meeting for coffee was a jolly affair. Everyone was talking and swapping experiences all at once. To their surprise it seemed that almost everyone could claim to have had some sort of meeting with God. Like Joan, they found it hard to put into words, and almost as hard to convey their feelings through drawing. But they felt sufficiently encouraged by their work so far to go home and explore their experiences further in full-sized paintings.

Before they left they agreed to hold an exhibition of the results in the church annexe the following Sunday and give a sort of summary of what they had learnt. The result, as Joan had hoped, was that a new awareness of the value and beauty of the church was born. Perhaps, thought Joan to herself, people will find that coming to terms with their church will lead them to enjoy their worship with a deeper sense of gratitude than before.

Notes

1. This story shows that these workshop ideas are not only valuable for those inside the church. They can all be adapted to suit the individual looking at the church from outside.
2. The results of one person's work often affect other people and encourage them to have a go.
3. The use of art often leads people towards the truth more accurately than a hundred well-chosen words.
4. Note how Joan, acting as the leader of the group, guided it towards answers that were relevant and useful. A good leader is there to throw out the red herrings.
5. Joan led the others from a position of personal experience. This is important. It is difficult to lead others to a place where you have not been yourself.
6. Religious experience is difficult to put into words. Mystics and poets have long struggled with the problem. Art has its own way of getting at the truth.
7. The exhibition was held in the church annexe. When we are still experimenting with ideas it is probably best to present them in places where they do not distract from the main focus of that place.

Episode Three: Sensing

James had just returned from a wonderful holiday in Italy where he had spent a lot of time visiting famous and beautiful churches. He was an enthusiastic photographer and had shot off rolls of film, concentrating particularly on religious art and architecture for which he had a special fascination. He had recently finished school and was about to go to university to study architecture.

He had enjoyed himself hugely in Italy but since his return he had begun to feel increasingly dissatisfied with his own church. Curiously enough, for one so interested in church buildings he was a member of a church which took pride in its lack of any form of outward embellishment. But then he'd been coming to this church for almost as long as he could remember and he had always liked its simplicity and lack of ostentation. Now, for the first time, he was unhappy with it. He sensed a lack of something in his surroundings that he could not define.

Personally things were going well for him. Why then was he not more glad to be back? As he lay in bed he began to remember some of the churches he had visited. While taking pictures in Italy he had been aware of something he wanted to capture on film, and when he looked through the photographs he had got back from the printers he could see that many of them had about them what he could only describe as a sense of mystery. It was something which he realised was entirely lacking in his own church.

While he was reflecting on this he remembered that he was going to a workshop that afternoon at his local camera club on 'Capturing an Atmosphere on Film'. The title had intrigued him. It was, after all, what he had been trying to do in Italy. Then an idea came to him: might not that mysterious atmosphere have been in his own church the whole time without his noticing it? How could he find out?

At that time of the morning in the church there would be no one about and he could experiment undisturbed. He dressed hurriedly and set off with camera and rolls of film. The door was unlocked. It occurred to him that he had never been in the church on his own at this time of the morning. It felt different. There was a buoyant, oddly welcoming atmosphere for such a silent place.

He sat himself in a pew and stayed there quietly for some time, hardly thinking, allowing the place to work its way into him. Then questions came to him. What am I doing here? What do I want to do? Yes, I came here because I wanted to see, to sense the atmosphere. Why? Quite unexpectedly he found himself answering his own question: 'Because I want to make sure I'm in the presence of God.'

He started taking pictures. He tried to capture his feelings about the place, but the mood changed. He ran through three reels of film and over three quarters of an hour went by. He sat down again and realised he was sitting in the place that he had spent the majority of his time photographing. It was his favourite spot. It was a place where he knew he could meet with God and be at peace in his presence.

Perhaps, he thought, he could mount an exhibition for the camera club, perhaps even for the church. If the pictures came out as well as he hoped he could arrange them in a way that might draw the attention of others to what he had experienced that morning. He might frame them and add a commentary as a guide.

If there was one particularly good one he would frame it and keep it on the wall over his desk at university to remind him of a place where he knew he could find God.

Notes

1. James's holiday had provided him with time to relax and assimilate a new range of thoughts and emotions. These had changed his perspective and encouraged him to grow spiritually. The result was a feeling of dissatisfaction. This is often a sign that we need to look again at the way we approach our faith. If we ignore our discontent we will slip into dullness. But if we take note of it and begin to ask questions there will be results. But we cannot know the answers before our search has begun.

2. The truth comes to us after we have paused and let our conscious thoughts slide into stillness. We can be too busy for our own good.

3. When you have been looking creatively you will know instinctively when the right answer is there. The answer comes easily when we have worked hard for it. It feels right when it feels natural and spontaneous.

4. Keeping reminders of your discoveries can be very helpful,

but they do have a limited life-span of usefulness. Creativity never stands still. Your discoveries must be used as starting off places for further discoveries, just as the ancient Polynesians colonised the Pacific by moving from island to island.

Episode Four: Accepting

Gwen had been having a recurring nightmare. She would dream that the whole world was at war and that she was running through the ruins of a bombarded city, calling out for her children and clutching something like a statue in her hands. Everywhere there was smoke and rubble, people crying out and screams. She seemed to have been running for ever, never getting anywhere, surrounded by devastation. This dream had been going on for the last few months and it was the sign of deep inner turmoil and pain.

Not so long before her husband had left her for another woman. Gwen, in her mid-forties, had been hit badly by this, even though, in some ways, it should have been a relief. Her husband George had for a long time had a problem with alcohol. It had never been easy to deal with and lately the situation had deteriorated.

But Gwen had loved George. She had done all in her power to help and protect him. Now she was on her own and although she wanted George to come back she knew in her heart that he had probably gone for ever. Now she was trying to come to terms with this.

Waking up from her nightmare she remembered that she had come home from church the previous evening carrying an empty vase. She had been intending to fill the vase with flowers which she would then put in the sanctuary for the Sunday morning service. On arriving home she had been distracted by an important telephone call and had forgotten all about the flowers.

Gwen was one of a small number of people in the church

who had the gift of making beautiful flower arrangements. It was her task along with others to keep the church bright with flowers at every season. She had a fine garden and it gave her pleasure to share what she could with the church. It was a kind of therapy for her, and a means of expressing her Christian commitment.

Recently, however, she had begun to have doubts about her role in the church. She was finding it difficult to relate to other church members who had not perhaps entirely understood her situation, though no criticism had been made openly of her conduct. She needed to re-evaluate her relationship with the church which she had been able to do through her flower arrangements. It was her way of answering all those hurtful questions which she felt were at the back of people's minds, and her own as well.

But the night before she had reached a crisis. That week she'd been asked by one of the other ladies if she could do all the flowers for the following Sunday as the rest of the regular team were going to be away. She had agreed without a second thought. But on arriving at the church on Friday evening with a large bunch of flowers in her arms she realised that she would have to work on arrangements for the altar and sanctuary as well. Previously she had always left these to the others and had concentrated on small arrangements for the more intimate corners of the church.

There was a reason for this. The experiences of her life had always made her reluctant to face the central fact of Christianity, that peace and love flowed out from the very heart of God and were available to all. The God she saw was responsible for the pain and rejection she had suffered. A flower arrangement in the sanctuary would have to deal directly with the sacrificial love of God, and this she could not understand or accept.

But by the time she had got to the sanctuary flower arrangement that Friday night she found she had run out of flowers. It might have been deliberate. In a panic she had picked up a vase from the vestry and rushed home to do them there. Then

the telephone had rung. It had been George, by turns incoher-
ent and abusive. After that she could not think about flower
arrangements.

It was now Saturday morning and still she had not done the
arrangement. Everyone would notice the absence of flowers in
the sanctuary if she failed to do anything. What should she do?
The telephone rang. Gwen picked it up expecting it to be a
hung-over and apologetic George. It turned out to be Janet,
the friend who normally did the flowers with her. She would
be home by lunch-time. Would Gwen like to come over and
take some flowers from her garden for the church?

Gwen's sense of relief was immediate and before she realised
what she was doing she was pouring out a torrent of pent-up
feelings that had been festering inside her for weeks. Janet
listened patiently and when there was a lull in Gwen's tirade
she suggested that they might have a cup of coffee and do the
flowers together.

After several cups of coffee Janet gently asked what Gwen
really wanted to do about the altar and sanctuary flowers. After
considering the question Gwen replied that she would consider
any idea that came but that what she most wanted to do was
to accept the environment. To Janet's question 'Why?' she
replied, 'Because I want to be at peace in it.'

Janet took Gwen into the garden to gather flowers. As they
were walking round Janet said that Gwen needed to come to
terms with her painful problems, and she could do so in terms
of a flower arrangement. Then she would at least have con-
fronted her difficulty, and perhaps have solved it.

They chose the flowers carefully to reflect all Gwen's
thoughts, then, after more coffee, they spent an unusually long
time over the arrangement until Gwen was fully satisfied. They
had lunch together.

The vase of flowers stood on the table. It represented a
whole array of emotions and ideas: anger, frustration, hurt,
loss, longing, love, sacrifice, redemption. Gwen began to reflect
on what she had achieved. She had been terrified when she

had arrived at Janet's house, scared that she was unloved and uncared for. But Janet had allowed her to see the real truth of her situation through a flower arrangement.

'All my emotions expressed here in these flowers,' said Gwen, 'when put together into a whole give me a sense of peace I haven't felt since childhood. The sufferings of Christ mirror my own. I feel consoled by this sense of sharing and unity. I will look forward to re-arranging these in the sanctuary at the foot of the altar. It will be a sign of my new-found acceptance.'

Notes

1. Not only can these workshops be effective for the individual or the group they can also be used as a form of counselling.
2. Some creative activities work better under certain conditions than others. For Gwen flower arranging is a soothing activity. Dance or drama would not have been appropriate in such a delicate situation.
3. Sometimes in workshops people appear to be completely at ease to begin with and then suddenly it is as if a storm has struck. This is not unnatural and should not cause alarm. A creative activity can bring deep-seated problems to the surface. It is important to deal with this calmly, to contain, to channel.
4. Janet calms Gwen first. Wordsworth said that poetry is emotion recollected in tranquillity. Janet gives Gwen time at every stage, allowing her to meet and accept her feelings, allowing her also to find her own answers.

Episode Five: Learning

Andrew had barely taken up his post as the new curate before his vicar began to persuade him to use his musical talents to build up a badly demoralised choir. There had been acrimonious disputes in the church before his arrival about the kind of music the church should have and the somewhat dictatorial approach of the choirmaster.

The congregation had expressed interest in new hymns and choruses but the choirmaster had kept on with a traditional diet of more classical fare. Eventually the choirmaster had left under a cloud taking with him half the choir and some of the congregation. The whole episode had been so bitter that, though its chief cause had now gone, harmony had not been restored. People on all sides of the argument were agreed on one thing: the affair had been handled very badly indeed.

So Andrew, the newcomer, was asked to sort it out. He was prepared to try, armed as he was with ignorance and the brash self-confidence of youth. But immediately he ran into seemingly immovable obstacles to progress. Forgiving and forgetting did not come easily to some members of the congregation. Andrew's enthusiasm was turning rapidly to despair. Then he remembered a series of seminars he had gone to at theological college.

At the time he had not taken them at all seriously. Subtle theological questions and the mastering of New Testament Greek took precedence. The seminars had formed part of a series of optional extra-mural studies. Now he thought that, as a last resort, he might try using some of the techniques he had learnt at them.

With great difficulty he managed to collect together all the people who had at some time expressed an interest in forming a new choir. They agreed to meet for a three-hour workshop on a Saturday afternoon in the church hall. Knowing that he had to begin from scratch, Andrew spent a good deal of time settling people down and relaxing them. Even this was not easy, but he persevered.

This accomplished, he then asked them what they all wanted to do. There was a longish silence. Several times he was tempted to break it but he remained quiet. Slowly answers began to come. Mostly they had to do with musical styles, how much the choir should sing, the use of musical instruments and so on. But Andrew was waiting for a deeper answer. Then someone mentioned that there was a special way one could learn about God through music. Andrew seized on this and brought it to everyone's attention. Not allowing anything to distract from this central issue he immediately asked why they should want to learn about God.

'It's obvious', 'It goes without saying', 'That's why we come to church', were the replies. But Andrew demanded more positive, direct answers. They became deeper. The answer that seemed to satisfy most of them was: 'in order to learn about love.'

'How can we achieve this through the medium of singing?' was Andrew's next question. This brought the workshop to a temporary standstill. Ideas were easy and stimulating to discuss. Practical solutions were harder to formulate and work out. But the prospect of achievement brought with it a certain excitement that had not been there before. They decided to write their own song which they would call 'Learning to Love'. They would set it to music of their own making. This was how they would discover the answer.

Andrew acted as a kind of chairman and referee, guiding their efforts along clear, unequivocal lines. There was a good deal of fun involved in making it rhyme, deciding on the number of verses, giving the piece a shape with a beginning, a middle and a rousingly satisfying conclusion. He kept them to their theme and allowed no distractions from it, however fascinating.

After a well-earned coffee-break they spent time polishing the piece and putting it into four part harmony. The result pleased them greatly. In reflecting on the workshop they realised that they had come from darkness into light. They had rediscovered that one of the reasons they came to church was to learn about God and to put the fruits of their learning to the test. It was something that had been missing in their worshipping lives.

'Learning to Love' became one of the standards in the reper-
tory of the new choir and Andrew's workshop was the beginning of a process in that church whereby theology and biblical
teaching were put into practice.

Notes

1. The church was divided over a very emotive issue. A creative workshop run by a natural leader was able to clear
   the way for healing and advancement.
2. If a church has a particularly difficult situation on its hands
   which might be answered by a creative workshop, the use
   of an impartial outsider often helps.
3. Andrew's enthusiasm was as important as his skills.
4. Time given to relaxation helped people begin the session
   with a fairly open mind. There are a number of books
   available on the subject of helping people relax. Or contact
   the SEEDS organisation.
5. Andrew was persistent in getting people to answer the
   questions he set accurately and positively. This established
   a disciplined and serious approach. It also gave the workshop a self-imposed direction.
6. The answers had to carry spiritual weight.
7. The third, most practical question required the most time
   before it was answered. And that time was allowed them.
8. Once they had broken the back of the problem they rested.
   Then they spent time polishing the results. It is important
   to have pride in your work.
9. They realised what had happened to them as a group when
   they reflected on what they had done.
10. They used this experience to take them forward into a
    brighter future. The experience had been one of redis-
    covering and regaining Paradise.

Episode Six: Understanding

Susie did not see herself as being religious even though she went to church. She had an enquiring mind that made it difficult for her to accept anything at face value. She was a potter, and though she had never had time to work as one on a full-time professional basis, she had great talent. Now that her family had grown up she was able to spend much of her time working in her little studio at home.

But though Susie prized her independence of thought her mind would constantly return to what she saw as the central truths of religion. Not long ago she had listened to a series of sermons on the beatitudes. She was struck by the way Christ's teaching was so simple yet possessing extraordinary weight and depth. The intellect alone could not grasp it.

It occurred to her that the beatitudes would provide a marvellous theme for a series of sculptures in clay. She had been looking for ways in which to express herself more fully in pottery and this seemed to be the answer. She put up a list of the beatitudes on the wall of her studio and started work. At first she made temporary little sculptures out of anything that came to hand. This helped her build up in her mind what the beatitudes meant to her. It was an exciting, exhausting process.

Having found the shape which fitted in with her understanding of the teaching she spent a day moulding it into a sculpture before firing it in the kiln. Then she painted and glazed it. The final result was spectacular.

Once a week Susie held a pottery class for some of the people in her church. A great deal of fun was had, gossip was exchanged and the occasional pot was thrown. On one of these evenings Susie revealed her new creation. It provoked a lively discussion and others decided to try their hand at something similar.

While Susie had been working on the project she had begun to realise that though she had come to some form of understanding about the beatitudes she still knew that she understood practically nothing about what lay behind each saying. Now she realised that her search for understanding had barely begun. What she needed to do was to look at each of the statements separately. She could do this with the class each week. They could meet for coffee first and meditate on each statement silently before working out its implications in a group discussion. Then they could turn to deciding how to translate their understanding into a sculptural form which would be accessible to others.

Eight happy and rewarding weeks were spent on each of the sayings. They followed Susie's practice of making a temporary structure out of anything that came to hand, then re-creating it in clay. At the end of eight weeks they held an exhibition. The pieces were placed strategically around the church, so that, without being too obtrusive, they would invite thoughtful consideration of the deeply enigmatic sayings they symbolised.

Notes

1. There are many levels on which this workshop can work. There is no need to go further than using a combination of objects.
2. One can go further however using a number of materials: clay, plasticine, wood, stone etc.
3. The group starts off the sessions meditating on the theme. All kinds of techniques can be used here, but the object is to focus and concentrate.
4. Susie allowed herself plenty of time to evolve her ideas for a group workshop.
5. They enjoyed themselves.
6. They not only acquired deeper understanding themselves, they were able to share that understanding with others, but in an unintrusive way, allowing those who viewed the objects to draw their own creative conclusions.

Episode Seven: Responding

Angie was a person full of life and ideas, but her ideas never became realities. She didn't regard herself as artistic, nor did she find it easy to express herself in practical terms. She envied people who had the gift to express themselves creatively and was prepared to have a go herself even when she thought she was no good at it.

Lately she had been going to keep fit classes. It had been very hard work at first, but she began to enjoy herself more and more. She took up tap dancing and an improvisatory jazz dance session once a week as well. What appealed to her was the sense of release she experienced through movement.

Angie went to the same church as Susie with whom she was great friends. When Susie had displayed the beatitudes' sculptures Angie had been one of the first to recognise the possibilities of a series of meetings to explore Susie's insights and understandings. With her enthusiasm it wasn't difficult for her to gather a group together.

At the first meeting Angie had asked what they wanted to do as a group. The answer for her was obvious: 'Respond to the teaching we've heard on the beatitudes with our whole being.' The answer to the second question, 'why?', also seemed clear. She wanted the teaching to be real for her. How was this reality to be achieved? Easy. Dance it.

The group began work. Suddenly the inspiration seemed to vanish and it became hard. Angie despaired until someone suggested they find some suitable music to start them off. It worked and before long they were deeply into a dance based on 'Blessed are the poor in spirit for theirs is the kingdom of heaven'.

It was still hard work. Inspiration came in fits and starts. A whole series of ideas expressed in movement were developed before there was a break to rest and recover. After the break they worked at polishing and at co-ordinating the sometimes disparate set of ideas that had been evolved.

They stopped again to reflect on how their work complemented that of Susie's group on the same theme. They realised that when they had completed work on all ten sayings they would have an entertainment to which they could invite members of the congregation. The approaches of sculpture and dance to the same theme of the beatitudes could be compared. Each would illuminate the other.

In addition to all this they realised that their response to the beatitudes had changed and matured in the most amazing way.

Notes

1. You don't have to be 'artistic' to have ideas, just enthusiastic.
2. There is nothing wrong in using the pattern of other people's workshops as a basis for your own. If the former have been successful it is a very good idea.
3. All it needs is the determination to have a go.
4. Ideas from one artistic medium can be translated into another.
5. Ideas can come from all kinds of sources. Observe, collect, be a magpie.
6. If the answers to questions are easy, hurry on to the next. There will always be a difficulty somewhere. When you find an obstacle don't give up.
7. Never leave a workshop unfinished. Make sure you bring it to a satisfactory conclusion. Do all you can to make it work and you will succeed more often than you think.

Episode Eight: Involvement

Ben was a joker. He liked to make people laugh. He was a man in his early forties with a family of four children. His job was setting up industrial displays which had its comic moments, but Ben really came into his own with children. He had a talent for involving people in an atmosphere of fun.

One weekend he took three of his children on a clowning course. The children had such a tremendous time that they decided to stage an evening's entertainment the following Saturday night for their eldest sister and their mother who had been unable to go along with them. They also agreed to invite some of their friends from the church, including the youth leader, and to make a real evening of it.

There was considerable debate as to what subject they should choose as their theme. The discussion and planning became more and more involved until it seemed as if nothing would be accomplished. Eventually Ben stepped in with the suggestion that maybe it would be a good idea to follow the theme for the following Sunday's service: 'Love one another as I have loved you.'

After initial bafflement and surprise this theme was agreed on. It was also thought to be a good idea to do the whole thing in mime. Every evening they got together for a couple of hours after supper to rehearse. They had decided to illustrate their theme through a series of funny incidents based on ones that had actually happened to them. Through clowning and mime they had to make them examples of how one can put the teachings of Christ into practice.

'Turning the other cheek' was made into a hilarious opening sequence, not entirely painless, however, for the participants. Then 'If someone asks you to walk a mile with him, walk two'; 'If someone asks for your coat, give him your shirt as well'; 'Forgive people seventy times seven, and more.' They had great fun and used their newly acquired knowledge to be endlessly inventive. All their props were imaginary, created through the medium of mime. They wore clown costumes and make-up, but made no use of scenery.

The whole of Saturday was spent getting it together so that it went like clockwork. The whole show was to last about twenty to twenty-five minutes, but it all went so well that

evening that, what with encores and lively audience partici-
pation, it lasted nearer an hour. By the end several people
were positively hurting with too much laughter.

It had been a great success, so much so that Felix, the
youth leader, suggested that they do a five-minute slot for the
congregation after the sermon at the Sunday morning service.

Ben and the children readily agreed. The following morning
Ben was dragged out of bed early by his children to rehearse
the shortened version and to correct certain things that hadn't
quite worked. They also devised a simple routine for the end
of their entertainment which would involve the whole congregation, bringing to life the commandment of loving one another
in a thought-provoking way.

Notes

1. Ben's family started with an art form they enjoyed. They
   did not necessarily start off being very good at it. But
   enjoyment is an excellent starting-point for any workshop.
2. In choosing the theme of 'loving one another' they were
   inevitably looking at the area of involvement in worship.
3. Had they sat down and asked themselves the question,
   'What do we want to do?', they would have answered, 'We
   want to practise what we have learnt.' If asked why, they
   could have answered, 'Because we want to be ready to
   practise what we've learnt in the outside world.'
4. It's wise to be simple.
5. They gave themselves plenty of time.
6. They polished their work.
7. They tested their results in an informal atmosphere.
8. They didn't think in terms of putting their entertainment
   into the church service. They were invited because what
   they'd done was thought to be a suitable aid to understanding, response and involvement in the life of church worship.
9. They didn't let success go to their heads. They adapted

their entertainment to the different conditions of the church.

10. Children can be an invaluable link in the process of learning to revitalise the life of a service.

Episode Nine: Celebration

Phyllis had been a member of the same church for longer than anyone could remember. She was in her eighties and was famous for bringing all sorts of little cooked goodies into the church every Sunday. She sold them after the service with coffee or tea for ridiculously small sums of money which she then put towards her favourite charities.

She had been doing this for years and felt that it was her way of contributing towards the happiness of the church and its outreach into the wider community. One Sunday the minister approached her and asked if she'd consider preparing a buffet-style lunch for the whole congregation after the service in a fortnight's time. He had planned to preach on the subject of celebrating the Christian message with thankfulness. He promised her that if she would accept he'd arrange for all the shopping to be done for her and for an army of helpers should she need them.

Phyllis's response to the minister's request was characteristically blunt: ''Course I will, so long as you pays for it. Don't you go giving me none of them young scallywags though. They don't want to do no work. My gals will look after me, don't you worry.'

The minister was delighted. He even bore with patient fortitude Phyllis's instructions on what he should include in his sermon so that she could prepare just the right sort of buffet to complement it. Phyllis began immediately to think about the menu, the minister's shopping list and whom she would choose to help her.

In the following two weeks Phyllis steadily organised the

whole operation. Every day one or two people would drop round to help her for an hour or so, then, three days before, they started in earnest. By the Saturday night they had everything together. It was a spread of which Martha in her kitchen in Bethany would have been envious.

On the Sunday morning Phyllis was up early putting the finishing touches to her work. At nine o'clock a battalion of helpers from the congregation were due to come and transport the results to the parish hall and she wanted to make quite sure she was ready for them.

Unlike Martha in the Gospels Phyllis was not bothered by many things and would never allow the distractions of the world to interfere with her religion, as she put it. Worship for Phyllis on a Sunday was sacrosanct and always came first. Everything had to be ready well in advance.

Needless to say the service and the lunch, which was really an extension of it, went marvellously well.

Notes

1. The structure for a possible workshop on celebration is well hidden in this illustration and needs to be drawn out by the reader.

2. The minister is the motivator behind the idea although he really doesn't participate except to suggest the idea and offer any extra help that might be needed. But he has done the groundwork by asking the questions, 'What do I want to do with this theme of celebration?' And he has answered the question by indicating to Phyllis that he wants the church to celebrate what they've all learnt in the sermon. To the question 'why' his reply would have been, 'Because the gift of love deserves celebrating.' How he achieved this is obvious. The point to note is that he involved other people in the process and let them get on with it.

3. In choosing Phyllis the minister knew that he could rely on her.

4. Phyllis has never been a professional cook, but that does not mean her skill is inferior. She is a better choice than a professional in many ways because she represents what the ordinary churchgoer can contribute to the celebratory life of their worship.
5. Phyllis is well-organised and spends time laying the foundations properly. She makes sure she knows what the theme is all about before starting.
6. She doesn't make the common mistake that Martha makes in the Gospels of being so busy that she leaves no time for worship. Worship is still the central act for her. Sometimes our enthusiasms or concerns take over and we lose sight of our ultimate object, the worship of God.

Episode Ten: Conclusion

Philip had been having a rough time. Two months ago he'd been given a month's notice to leave his job. He had been working with a company for several years doing research but he had come to feel that many of the things he was being asked to do were unethical. It had caused him a lot of heart-searching until one day he had decided to speak his mind. His criticisms had not gone down well, and when he had begun to mount a public campaign he had been given the sack.

He had felt bitter about his dismissal and did not think he had been treated at all fairly. Then, two weeks after this, his fiancée told him she didn't want to marry him and promptly went off with one of his best friends. Understandably he was at a low ebb. People in the church had been marvellous. They had supported him in every way they could. One person in particular, a girl called Marie, helped him to see that becoming bitter towards God, the world and everything in it would do him no good at all.

All the same, he found going to church on Sunday extremely difficult and, had he not been the only organist available, he would definitely have stayed away. One of his few consolations was thundering away on the organ which helped to exorcise some of his feelings. But it was not long before comments were made that he might perhaps consider playing some gentler music.

Marie suggested that he might use the sermons as themes for playing music which expressed something of what he had learnt and felt. He said he'd try the following week.

Strangely enough, he found that listening to the service in this way had made him think very hard about what it all meant to him. It had been a challenge to sum up the service in a five-minute toccata and fugue. What had proved an even greater challenge had been the vicar's theme of forgiveness and healing which had been based on the story of the leper in Mark's Gospel.

Philip had had to concentrate hard to find a fitting conclusion to the service. He had to bring all the strands together in a way that was truthful to his own experiences. He managed it, not to his own musical satisfaction, but well enough for several members of the congregation to come up to him after the service and congratulate him on his sensitive playing.

Notes

1. The re-creation of our experiences, however painful, through a medium that demands creative discipline which can then be turned into worship is invaluable.
2. The therapy that Marie suggests for Philip contains all the elements that a good creative workshop needs.
3. Philip's problems could have barred him from finding salvation for himself and others.
4. Marie's suggestion gently persuades him to channel his feelings creatively.
5. The undisciplined emotions expressed in just thundering away don't get us any further than letting off steam. They

are evidence of self-pity and can be as embarrassing for the witness as they are futile to the sufferer.

6. The concentration required to answer the questions, 'What is it all about?', 'Why?' and 'How can we sum it up in a way that will make it effective?', is enormous. It is a creative discipline in its own right. But the benefits are correspondingly great. They richly reward both the participants and the bystanders.

Episode Eleven: Stewardship

Harry was in his late fifties. He had entered the ministry in his thirties after a career in industry. He had recently taken on a group of run-down churches to look after. He wondered if he'd done the right thing. He liked a challenge but he realised that restoring life to each of these churches would be a hard task. Perhaps it was a younger man's job.

But Harry was well-organised and knew how to delegate responsibility. It was not long after he had taken on this new assignment, though, when he realised he would need all his old managerial skills to realise his vision of a thriving group of largely self-supporting churches. The task was daunting. There were five churches in all, and virtually no one to draw on for support. It seemed as if he would have to do it on his own.

But Harry had another great gift. He could tell stories really well, in particular children's stories. It wasn't long before people began to come to the churches with their children for the stories he told in his sermons. The news of Harry spread. His churches were now well-attended, but no one was doing much to help with Harry's ministry.

Then, one Sunday, Harry began to embark on a series of stories which had a very particular theme to them, stewardship. Harry had prepared the ground very carefully. He had spent many weeks writing a series of stories that everyone would enjoy listening to, and yet, as the stories progressed, the point was made increasingly clear that he could not go on serving five churches unless he received adequate support from his followers.

Such was the power of his stories that it was hard for his hearers not to offer their support. He made it clear that everyone had something to contribute, however small, and that a happy community depended on good creative worship which in turn depended on good stewardship.

It took Harry several weeks to tell this series of stories, but by the end of them most people had got the point. From then on Harry's managerial skills came into their own. He used the harvest of his sermons as a basis for his vision of self-governing churches. From then onwards his ministry could become freer and more personal.

It took several years to accomplish, but by the time he was due for retirement he had achieved his goal and had acquired sufficient leisure to allow him to put his stories into a couple of books.

Notes

1. Harry had a special need. In the worship of his churches he lacked one vital ingredient: good stewardship. Without that the creative and redeeming life of the churches couldn't really get under way. Sometimes it is only one ingredient in worship that needs attending to for all the rest to fall into place. It is wise to consider this point before embarking on a whole series of changes that need not be made if the key problem is solved first.

2. Harry didn't have any resources to hand before embarking on this extended form of workshop. By the end he had all the resources he needed.

3. The theme of his stories followed on from his creative questioning. What do I need? Answer: Help to make the communal act of worship function properly. Why? Because in order

for it to work everybody needs to play their part. How to achieve this? Through the creative use of story-telling.
4. Harry planned the operation carefully in advance.
5. Through story-telling the points were made effectively and painlessly. The pill was sugar-coated and gave pleasure.
6. He allowed the stories to do their own work.
7. He harvested the results.

Episode Twelve: Outreach

Meg had not been a Christian for that long and, like a lot of people new to Christianity, she was very keen to join in. As a teacher she felt she had a lot to offer the church, given the opportunity. Her interest lay in the outreach of the church to the world. As a teacher of English and Drama she was aware of the issues that affected children. It was these very issues that she felt needed to be pursued in the life of the church.

She was in her late twenties and her eagerness to explore the issues of justice and peace was very strong. One of the reasons she had become a Christian was the quality of friendship she had experienced in her local church. Her one criticism was that it was inclined to be inward looking. It wasn't that members of her church didn't care about what was happening in the outside world, but no one seemed to want to be involved in what was happening. She felt the need to encourage the church to respond to world issues. But how could she achieve this without upsetting people unduly?

Whenever she mentioned the subject the response was luke-warm. 'We do have intercessions and prayers, you know' or 'I think we've got enough to worry about within our own community'. There had been plans to start various projects but no one ever had the time or inclination to follow them through.

Meg decided to hold some workshops similar to those she had led with her pupils at school. Whatever they were studying in History and Geography she would encourage them to look at from a dramatic point of view. It often achieved excellent results with them, why not with the church?

It troubled her that so much attention should be given to receiving, sharing and celebrating the love of God and so little to those who needed it most, beyond the confines of her well-ordered parish. Surely the message of love was so important it needed to be shared with the whole world? Wasn't that the meaning of the hymn they loved to sing: 'Let all the world in every corner sing, my God and King'?

Meg wanted to develop her ideas with a group that met on Saturdays, or perhaps on a weekday evening. Through improvising on subjects which they had studied they could re-create situations which would provide them with clues to help them reach out to the needy.

The story of the Good Samaritan kept coming into her mind. Chad Varah had been inspired by the story to start the Samaritan organisation; perhaps that could be a starting-point for exploring how the story applies to everyday life. A series of dramatic improvisations could be used to make the parable vivid and significant. Meg believed she had a calling to start this work.

She began quietly with a group of young people in the church. It was in a way an extension of her work at school. But the limitations imposed on her by the secular and compulsory atmosphere of the school were not with her here. She could dare much more with a group of people who were willing to enter on a journey with her which could have far-reaching personal consequences.

The group consisted of no more than four or five to begin with. Between them and Meg an atmosphere of complete trust was established very quickly. Each member of the group felt able to try out all kinds of ideas. Using the Good Samaritan as their foundation they explored new situations each week until they found a theme which grabbed everyone's interest. The theme was homelessness.

Together and individually they found out all sorts of facts

about homelessness. They first looked at their own locality, then at the country, finally at the situation in the world as a whole. By the time they had taken in the global picture they felt fairly depressed by what they had discovered.

Undaunted, Meg took them on to the next stage of improvisation. Having found out what they were interested in and after exhausting the question 'Why?' she led them on to the question of how something practical could be done to alleviate the problems they had unearthed.

Every week they improvised all kinds of possible solutions. Then one evening they suddenly realised that one of these was something in which they themselves could actually be involved. It was easy enough to put the burden of responsibility on governments and big institutions, but it was a humbling, though at the same time inspiring experience, to realise that they too had something to contribute. They too could help to build the Kingdom of Heaven on earth. Then they remembered that the original parable was an answer to a simple but profoundly practical question: 'Who is my neighbour?'

Through a whole series of improvisations the group had moved from ignorance to knowledge, from indifference to concern, from inaction to action. As they started to implement the results of all this work through a programme of intercession, affiliation with organisations already at work in the field and a local project, other members of the church began to show interest. After a period of only two years Meg had helped to transform the outlook of a loving but introverted church into a loving and caring church whose horizons were as limitless as the round world itself.

Notes

1. Meg, a new member of the church, had seen a gap in the church's worship. We can often learn about shortcomings from a relative outsider or beginner.

2. Meg didn't rush in. She gave herself time for prayerful consideration.

3. She wanted to make sure of her professional experience, but quite rightly made sure that she wasn't putting her desires before God's.

4. She realised that her style of workshop could lead to people's imaginations prompting them to actions that could have a great effect for good. This was no pipe-dream because everything was based on the word and inspiration of Christ.

5. Meg was eager but prepared to wait. Waiting for God's approval is essential to the success of a project like this.

A Workshop

This is an example of a workshop that is being used to help a church group understand their Sunday worship. This is done by looking at what the formal words of their service are saying to them through the creative medium of drama. This helps them to find out, and accept, the layout of their service, take it to heart, and let it enlighten them with its internal truth and light.

DRAMA WORKSHOP LEADER Let's start off this workshop by asking the question: 'What does the Introduction to Worship mean to us?'

PHILIP It means the beginning of worship.

W.L. When is the beginning of worship?

PHILIP The moment you enter the church.

W.L. Does that constitute the Introduction to Worship?

ANGELA No. I think the Introduction to Worship is when the leader of the service comes in.

W.L. Any other ideas?

NORMAN I think the Introduction to Worship occurs when the first words are spoken.

ELAINE When the music starts.

JOHN When there is a sense of silent anticipation.

PIPPA It's about starting off on the right foot. (*Laughter*)

NORMAN Which foot, the right or the left?

PIPPA Exactly. It's about knowing which foot to start off on and then starting off on it!

ELAINE I think that's when the music starts.

ANGELA　But how can the music tell us which foot we need to start off with?

W.L.　It all really depends on what we mean by starting off on the right foot, doesn't it? Are we being literal?

JOHN　No, of course not. The Introduction to Worship involves everyone knowing what it is they are involved in.

W.L.　How is that achieved?

JOHN　Through an announcement or a general understanding.

ANGELA　Everyone knows that the Sunday morning service follows a particular pattern.

W.L.　Should we take it for granted that we know what is going to happen?

PIPPA　Well if we don't nothing can happen.

W.L.　Then does the Introduction to Worship set the tone for the rest of the service?

ANGELA　Yes.

PHILIP　Yes, it should and I think it happens in a number of different ways. There is the music, there are people entering, there is the formal start to the service, which may be set in motion by the choir or the priest or someone else.

W.L.　Is it important for us to know what is going to happen or do we just leave that all to the leader of the service?

PHILIP, ANGELA, JOHN, ELAINE　It's important for all of us to know.

W.L.　So perhaps the Introduction to Worship may be stretched to mean that there are various points in the service where the leader lets the others know what is coming next?

NORMAN　No, I think the Introduction is at the beginning only.

W.L.　But perhaps in the Introduction there is a theme which is elaborated on throughout the service, rather like the prologue to a play which hints at what's to come. For example, in Shakespeare's *Henry V* the Chorus starts the play off and then keeps coming back in at various points to comment on what's going on.

What does the Introduction to Worship mean to us?
1. The beginning of worship.
2. The moment we enter a church.
3. When the leader of a service comes in.
4. When the first words of a service are spoken.
5. When the music starts.
6. When there is silence.
7. Starting off on the right foot.
8. Knowing what is going to happen.
9. An announcement that it has begun.
10. A general understanding that it has begun.
11. Setting the general tone.
12. A formal commencement.
13. A prologue.
14. A chorus.
15. A guide to what is going to happen next.

W.L.   From six people we have got a huge array of ideas. Can we choose just one of these to work on?

JOHN   Knowing what is going on.

W.L.   Is everyone happy with that? Then let's ask the question, 'Why do we want to know what is going on?'

ELAINE   Because we want to join in.

ANGELA   Because there would be chaos if we didn't.

W.L.   Would there be chaos?

ANGELA   Yes of course. If no one introduces the next hymn then how can people hope to start singing it? It's bad enough trying to get people to respond as it is but if there was no form of leadership then nothing would happen.

W.L.   Is this true?

ANGELA   Show me a service where it wouldn't be.

W.L.   So the clearer the Introduction the better the response?

ANGELA   Yes, I should say so.

JOHN   People need to be led. The leader is like a shepherd with a flock of sheep, they need to be told what to do and driven to it by the sheepdog.

W.L.   That sounds pretty cynical. Don't you think a congregation is capable of guiding itself?

PIPPA   Certainly not. If it tried, the result would be the chaos Angela talked about.

W.L.   So congregations aren't to be trusted?

PIPPA   No, it's not a question of lack of trust, it's a question of guidance. As soon as you get a large group of people together you need to have someone leading them, partly because there is such a divergence of opinion, as we have here. Without a leader no direction is chosen, and nothing is achieved.

W.L.   Which brings us back to the need we have at different points in a service to be made aware of what is about to happen. So the Introduction to Worship is not something that just happens at the start of a service. It is something that needs to happen at various stages in a service if we are to worship together lovingly and effectively as a group.

NORMAN   We have to be united in worship.

W.L.   Yes for reasons already stated.

JOHN   We need markers that show us where we are or where we have come from and where we're going to.

W.L.   Yes. So to sum up:

Why do we want to know what is going on?
1. We want to join in.
2. We want to prevent chaos.
3. We need to be led.
4. We need to be told what to do.
5. We need to be united.
6. We need to know where we are.

W.L.   Can we put all these answers into one sentence?

ANGELA   We want to worship together as a united group of Christians.

W.L.   Everyone agree? Now we move on to the practical question of how we can use the Introduction to Worship to help us to worship together as a united group of Christians.

We are here because we are all interested in using drama to help us take a fresh look at our worship. How can we use drama to bring us together as a united family? Let's suppose we are a group of people who want to stage a play. How do we start?

ELAINE   We choose a play.

W.L.   What play are we going to choose?

PIPPA   Do you mean a real play or a service of worship?

W.L.   A service of worship can be seen as a sort of play.

JOHN   I suggest we take our main Sunday service.

W.L.   All agreed? Good. Does the service have a particular script to it?

PHILIP   What do you mean script?

W.L.   A particular liturgy.

ANGELA   Excuse me, but I've never been quite sure what people mean when they talk about liturgy.

W.L.   It is the form of words used in a particular service. It is the framework and substance of a service in the same way that a script is for a play. Of course there are services that have little or no apparent liturgy to them at all. These could be described as free services, though freedom in this respect is a tricky concept. Freedom can only be truly expressed within understood and accepted boundaries. Do we have a liturgy?

NORMAN   Yes, of sorts.

W.L.   What does that mean?

NORMAN   Well, there are all sorts of variations to it. It's difficult to know what it is.

W.L.   Let's choose one variation and explore it just as we would do a play. Let's start by reading it together.

. . .

Do we understand it?

ANGELA   Yes.

PHILIP   Not all of it. I don't understand what the 'apostolic church' means.

W.L.   How do we find out?

ELAINE   Look in a dictionary.

PIPPA   A Church dictionary.

W.L.   How about trying to puzzle it out from our knowledge of what the word apostle means?

. . .

W.L.   Are there any other things we don't understand?

. . .

W.L.   Does it produce any emotional response in us?

PIPPA   Yes.

JOHN   No.

PIPPA   It makes me want to cry and it also makes me want to shout out 'Hallelujah'.

JOHN   It doesn't make me want to do either. It leaves me numb, but I do come away from it with a knowledge of having done – how can I put it? – of having been in the right place.

W.L.   You come away feeling satisfied?

JOHN   Yes. In a way. Satisfied and unsatisfied. It's a complicated feeling.

W.L.   So it does produce an emotional response, though not one that you easily recognise?

JOHN   I suppose it does, yes.

W.L.   Let's read it again only this time concentrating on our emotional response to the text.

. . .

W.L.   What are our reactions?

PIPPA   They're varied.

NORMAN   It's difficult to define the feelings.

PHILIP   It felt richer, more meaningful.

W.L.   Now let's look at how this text introduces our worship to us. Can you see where it acts as a presenter? It has a way of presenting us with the next step to be undertaken. It shows us what direction we need to take and how to take it. It invites us to share in the experience together,

(*The whole of this section takes a considerable amount of time to work through. It is the practical part of the workshop. Ideas are worked out and fully experienced through the medium of drama.*)

I want you each to choose a section and work on the words until you feel you can present them in a way that carries all the feeling they can contain.

Do you need to use gestures?

Do you need to learn it off by heart?

Do you need to speak the lines from a particular spot?

Is there room for a dialogue, or for lots of voices?

Should it be done as choral speech?

Do you mean what you are saying?

Does the meaning come across?

Who are you speaking to?

If you are addressing an unseen presence are your words as meaningful as if you were addressing one of the members of this workshop?

Philip, do you believe Elaine's words?

Do you fully understand them?

Do they move you in any way?

Come on Elaine, try again.

What are the words saying?

What are they doing?

What response do you want from them?

Use Pippa as a sounding board.

Now use Norman – Angela – John.

Now use everyone.

Now address your words to God.

Do they ring true?

Are they full of meaning, full of feeling?

Who is this God you are talking to?

What is this God like?

Where is God?

Now say the words again.

Go on saying them until you know them inside out.

Use your own words.

Mime them.

Use pure sound to convey your meaning.

Use the names in a telephone directory to convey the feeling.

Go on practising alone – with each other – with the group until you finally succeed in becoming real, until you believe with your whole being that what you are saying is true.

Now start again and introduce your section of worship as a team.

What's the difference?

ANGELA Commitment.

PHILIP Excitement.

PIPPA Yearning.

ELAINE Longing.

NORMAN Feeling.

JOHN I felt that God was really in our midst.

W.L. Is it scary?

ELAINE Early on, a little, yes.

W.L. And now?

ELAINE Not at all, it's as though there were a buzz inside me. I feel warm and alive.

W.L. Yes?

ALL Yes.

PIPPA Something has happened which I'd like to spend more time exploring.

W.L. Good. Yes. Every Sunday morning. Explore, live, feel and know that God is here.

6

A Creative Weekend

The Team
The Leader: Paul
Dance: John
Music: Peter
Art: Yvonne
Drama: Reggie

The Aim
1. To revitalise the church's Sunday morning worship.
2. To provide an original evening service.

The Creative Catalysts
Art, Drama, Music and Dance

PAUL This is the layout for the weekend. We need to arrive at the church by 5.00 p.m. at the latest on Friday night. We'll be met by members of the church who will then show us around the building and the rooms we shall be working in. After that we'll be taken to the homes where we are staying for the weekend. At 7.30 p.m. we'll gather in the church hall to meet everyone taking part in the weekend. This will be the introductory session which will involve a general look at the programme to start people thinking creatively. I'll introduce the theme and then John will take over for a warm up session. This will end at 9.30 p.m.

Saturday morning we'll split into groups. John, you'll be in the church hall with the dance group. They've got a piano and a pianist and a record player available for you. Peter, you'll be in the vestry with the music group. They've got all sorts of instruments for you to work with, as well as a piano. Yvonne, the art group will be in the pastor's house. They've got a large empty room and there'll be all the paints, pencils, crayons, paper and other things there that you've requested. Reggie, you'll be in the school gymnasium which is next door to the church. I'll be in the church itself. The Saturday morning session will begin after prayers in the church at 9.30 a.m. This session lasts until 11.45 a.m. when there will be a coffee break until 12.00. The second session is from 12.00 until 1.15 p.m. when we'll all break for a sandwich lunch. Lunch will be provided for us.

The third session will be from 2.30 until 4.00 p.m. with tea from 4.00 to 4.30 and then session four will be from 4.30 until 5.45 when we'll break for prayer in the church. After that we'll be taken by our hosts, to have supper in their homes. At 8.00 p.m. we're all going to meet again in the hall for a party.

Sunday morning we hope the work will transform the quality of the service. The service will start at 10.30 a.m. and finish by midday. After the service we'll be having lunch with our hosts. At 2.30 p.m. we'll go on to session five where we'll be exploring new approaches to worship. This session will go on until 4.00 p.m. The sixth session will be from 4.30–6.00 which will be a technical rehearsal for the evening worship, where we'll be putting it all together. Our new, free form of worship will be from 6.30 until 7.30 p.m.

Any questions so far?

JOHN   Am I going to have to contend with tea trollies all day in the hall?

PAUL   No, sorry, there is a separate area for the kitchens and there is a large common room next to them. You'll be quite free of all that.

JOHN   Thank you. Oh, and is there heating in the hall and will it be on?

PAUL   Yes, I'll see to that.

PETER   Can I swop with you at some point so that we can use the organ?

PAUL   Yes, of course.

YVONNE   Are we a long way off from everyone else?

PAUL   No, just next door.

YVONNE   Is there enough light in the room?

PAUL   Yes, it's got huge windows facing south, I think. Let's look at the layout for the sessions. So far we're decided that you, Yvonne, should tackle the first three elements of worship: inspiration, searching and sensing. Reggie, you'll be dealing with accepting, learning, understanding; Peter with responding, involvement and celebration, and John with conclusion, stewardship and outreach.

PETER   Paul, what are you going to be doing?

PAUL   I will be covering some of the same ground as Reggie. There are a lot of different aspects to learning that we need to look at if we are going to provide the church with a comprehensive survey of their worship.

   I'll be concentrating on the sermon, the lessons and the liturgy.

PETER   Fine by me.

PAUL   We've got four sessions of about one to one and a half hours in which to cover three elements of worship each. Can we do it?

EVERYONE   No.

PAUL   How much can we cover properly in that time?

YVONNE   Two elements at the most.

REGGIE   By the time we've got used to each other, you know, played some games to break down people's reticence and then asked all the questions – and it takes longer to get answers from people than you think – we shall be hard pushed to cover two of the elements of worship properly.

PETER   I agree.

PAUL Well, we will have had the general get-together on the Friday night to help us get used to one another and during that initial session we can introduce the idea of asking and answering questions.

REGGIE Yes, but they'll still need a good deal of encouragement next morning.

PAUL I think we can cover two elements quite well in the time given in four sessions. Perhaps we could scrap the party and use that time for an extra session.

REGGIE That is an appalling suggestion.

PAUL If we cut the party down to one hour would that give us time?

YVONNE It might just.

PAUL We'll ask them to let us have from 8.00–9.00 p.m. for a further session and then to meet all together for a shorter party. Actually I think that makes better sense because the party should go with more of a swing. We'll be able to maintain our momentum.

So during the induction on Friday evening I'll introduce the whole subject of creativity in worship and present the theme for the weekend which is going to be 'Epiphany'. We'll get everyone used to the idea of asking and answering questions by having a question and answer session on 'What is Epiphany?', 'Why Epiphany?' and 'How can we make Epiphany as meaningful as possible?' After that John will take over with a dance session where we will be learning a couple of dances involving the idea of Epiphany. All this material will come in useful for the experimental Evening Service.

During session one on Saturday morning I suggest you start by getting your groups well used to the whole process of creative questioning. The afternoon sessions should then be far easier to set in motion especially as we are not moving groups round from one workshop leader to another. I guess that by the time you have reached 9.00

p.m. you will have covered the ground. That will leave an hour to release all the tensions with a party.

On Sunday morning we start with the usual morning worship of the church, and I hope that will have a feeling of being completely fresh.

We have two aims here. First we want to ensure that everyone experiences a sense of release when involved in those elements of worship that they have been working on. Secondly, they should experience a sense of release in others when they see the results of what they have been working on. But nobody should feel their form of worship has been tampered with in any way.

By the time we come to session five we should have gathered enough material for the experimental service in the evening. What we need to do in this session is gather together all the work we have done and revise, polish and lick it into shape. For example if you, John, have designed an Epiphany dance in our general get-together we can use that as well as the other work you have done during the five sessions. Peter, I'm sure you will have concocted some Epiphany music and perhaps a choral piece that we can use. Reggie, I know you will have got together some drama material that will be valuable and Yvonne's group are bound to have produced a variety of work based on the Epiphany scene; banners perhaps? I will have produced some interpretive work with the sermon, lessons, prayers and liturgy which can also be used.

Session Six we'll meet in the church and quickly sort the material into an order of presentation. It will be a sort of technical rehearsal.

Then into the experimental service. I think it would be wise to start in stillness to give us a time to centre down. Otherwise it will just become a chaotic jamboree. Yvonne, we'll need your group's expertise in devising some large banners on which to place the running order for everyone to see. Any questions?

JOHN   Will there be any form of follow up?

PAUL   Yes, we will have a meeting with the church at a later date to discuss the results. We'll also be bringing the completed video along for viewing.

PETER   So we may be coming back to the church for further workshops in the future?

PAUL   If they want us back, yes. It is possible that they may want us to combine with other churches in the area to form a large group that will meet at a conference centre for the weekend. That seems to be a popular way of combining resources. Good luck.

This is an approximate reconstruction of a Seeds Creative Workshop weekend that was held at Holy Trinity Church in Knaphill in Surrey. As a consequence of that workshop we were asked back the following year to conduct a special Sunday evening service on the theme of Pentecost. The church was packed, and about four hundred people took part.

Seeds is involved in many similar situations around the country, working with individual churches and groups of churches as well as with clergy, post ordination training and mid-service training and in theological colleges.

This approach to creative worship has proved to be very successful for all the churches we have worked with because it provides congregations with the opportunity of being involved in a project which is of mutual concern. It provides the churches with a feeling for mission, both internal and external. It produces a lot of laughter and good will. Relationships are deepened, and this can only help the church to grow and mature in its vision for the future. If you are interested in knowing more about this aspect of Seeds do please contact us and we will be only too willing to help you.

7

A New Service

It might be thought that creating new forms of worship is more exciting than renovating already existing services but I don't think this is true. It is relatively easy to create new forms of worship but it is also just as easy to get bored with them because they have a tendency to be shallow. This is not to dismiss the importance of exploring new approaches. I am in favour of innovation but not at the expense of throwing away what has been found valuable and nourishing over the years. We need to find a balance between the old and the new. In this way what no longer works can be replaced with something that makes sense for our present-day needs.

I am not the person to say what is or isn't relevant. That is for the church to decide. But to discard the old for the new purely for the sake of change is folly. To transpose the words of Pope:

> For forms of worshipping let fools contest,
> Whatever works the best for us is best.

If our faith is challenged by new forms of worship so much the better. Faith would not be faith unless it were able to stand up to the pressure and turmoil of change.

We need to explore because we need to keep on hearing about God. God's creativity can appear to be so elusive. But he delights in his creation and asks us to join in his delight by being creative in our response.

I haven't attempted in this book to set aside a section on creating new services because there are plenty of people cur-

rently providing material for such services. It has been my task
to help rejuvenate existing services. However in this chapter I
would like to provide an example for those who want to explore
worship in new directions.

In life it isn't possible to create new work without first imitat-
ing and learning from what already exists. If we try to create
new services of worship without first learning to understand
the worship we already have then all we shall be doing is
throwing the baby out with the bath water. We will create
pastiches which have no heart to them.

The purpose of worship is to expose the heart to an emotional
and spiritual response. When you fall in love you don't die of
boredom you die of yearning, yearning to express your
emotions. Worship is just the same. We long to express our
feelings to God. Once we realise that formal worship contains
the means to express these feelings we have a choice. Do we
rekindle the worship that already exists, or do we need to find
new ways of worshipping God?

I believe that most people profit from participating in both.
Involving ourselves in new forms of worship can provide us
with an exciting way of rediscovering old truths. But I am wary
of experimentation that loses sight of its roots. That is why I
have concentrated on worship as it exists.

Having explored formal worship patterns as far as I can I
now believe that it is possible to look at new forms of worship.
New ideas for worship spring directly out of our understanding
of worship as a whole. Worship is inherently a creative and
artistic act. It calls for, indeed needs, the contribution of all
the creative disciplines that are to be found in everyday life.
Once the right questions have been asked it isn't difficult to
provide the right answers. The difficulties arise when we try to
put these answers into practice.

During the creative weekend the workshops produced plenty
of material to provide an evening service that could truly be
called new and original. At the same time these workshops

also supplied insights that gave the formal service of worship a new-found glow and vibrancy.

It would be very difficult to describe the difference that these workshops had made to the morning service. The evidence of renewal was obvious to those taking part. The Spirit of God was almost tangibly present. Yet the service, to all outward appearances, was no different to what it had previously been. The only visible sign of a difference I can remember on this particular occasion was when the vicar was moved to use his whole body in a sweeping circular gesture, hands outstretched, to express the feeling of a prayer that embraced the whole world. It was significant, in being unusual, and yet it was absolutely right for that moment. It was in fact the free expression of heartfelt worship that had been allowed to come alive through movement. In a service of formal worship this was a remarkable and beautiful sight. But in the freer creative atmosphere of the experimental evening worship evidence of greater flexibility pervaded the service.

Here is an impression of what it was like.

To start with the church was festooned with banners, paintings and sculptures that drew our attention to the theme of Epiphany. The entrance to the church proclaimed the fact that we were entering the temple of light. It was alive with candles, lanterns, torches, stars and paintings. Inside were gathered as many different forms of light as we could find, dotted all round the church. The banners and paintings proclaimed that Christ had come into the world to turn our darkness into light, our hate into love, our imprisonment into freedom, our doubt into faith. The service started with an Epiphany dance. This had been put together on the Friday evening. It was devised to express the idea of bringing the light of Christ into the world. This meant letting everyone know it was there. We could have developed the idea in a number of ways. We could have used the church like a map of the world and had everyone spreading out to every corner with candles and Bibles and songs of praise. As it was the whole congregation was dancing and singing its way round the church. This gave the event a sense of carnival so alien to the English temperament and yet so appropriate to a religious festival.

When people had finally settled themselves in pews, chairs, on the floor, by the heaters and on the window ledges we quite naturally moved on to a liturgical dance. Those who had been involved in dance applied their experience by finding movements appropriate to 'the transporting of the light to all the world'. This was accompanied by the singing of the hymn 'Come Holy Ghost our souls inspire'. Normally people wouldn't dream of allowing themselves the freedom to experiment with their feelings through movement, but here it became quite natural, in fact a necessity. It was as if the prayer of outreach to the world had to be expressed in this way.

When this part of the worship had come to an end there was silence. The rhythm of our worship had required stillness after action. As happens in Quaker meetings this continued until people needed to express themselves in vocal prayer. Prayers now became genuine calls for help or expressions of gratitude or remembrance. Prayers were expressed through paintings people had done, poems people had written, through mime, through dance and through music.

Once more the natural rhythm of worship brought us back to a stillness where we were ready to listen again. There was a reading from Revelation 21 in which the city of God was described as being lit by the Lamb. This was movingly illustrated by the presence of hurricane lamps surrounding the reader in the centre of the darkened church. The reading had become a dramatic re-enactment of light bursting forth into the world with the presentation of Christ in the temple and the spreading of the word. Added to this was a reading from 'The Rock' by T. S. Eliot, a poem about the church and its function as a means of conveying the light of Christ:

Therefore we thank Thee for our little light, that is dappled with shadow.

We thank Thee who hast moved us to building, to finding, to
   forming at the ends of our fingers and beams of our eyes.
And when we have built an altar to the Invisible Light, we may
   set thereon the little lights for which our bodily vision is made.
And we thank Thee that darkness reminds us of light.
O light invisible, we give Thee thanks for Thy great glory!

This led into the creed which had been worked on as a
piece of choral speaking and as a musical composition involving
initially a group of twenty people. It ended up with everyone
taking part. After this there was a sermon in which a number
of people shared their reflections on Epiphany dramatically
while others described what it had come to mean for them
through their paintings. Some of the dancers explained the
thoughts on Epiphany that they had discovered and were
expressing through dance.

The service ended with a great burst of communal singing.
Nothing could have been more suitable to the mood of thanksgiving and sheer enthusiasm than George Herbert's great
hymn: 'Let all the world in ev'ry corner sing my God and King'.

If the morning service possessed the majesty that is necessary
for the principal expression of a church's worship, the evening
service provided the right counterbalance by being full of all
the exuberance and bursting passion appropriate to the celebration of some of the great Christian themes such as
Epiphany. The knowledge that this great festival could be cele-
brated twice in one day in such different ways made me realise
the great truth that the creativity of God knows no boundaries.
New forms of worship, fresh approaches to creativity, are
entirely possible and desirable when the old meets the new and
when the new springs out of the old. The rock upon which our
faith is founded can be struck again and again to produce the
fresh and abundant water of life.

8

Putting It All Together

When I had my first car I remember thinking how fascinating it would be to take the whole thing apart and then see if I could put it all together again so that the car would go better than it had before. It really doesn't take a lot of intelligence to do the first. The troubles start to occur when you try to put it all back again.

I can just see myself now, surrounded by a thousand different bits of metal wondering how on earth they fitted together. I had been very careful about dismantling every section, making sure that I had written down how each piece was fitted to the next, and yet when it came to reversing the process nothing seemed to fit any more. It resembled the experiences of potholing where no matter how careful one had been to register the direction of one's forward explorations, when it came to retracing one's movements everything looked entirely different. If it hadn't been for the extended thread of string or the chalk marks on the walls one would have been hopelessly lost and only rescued by someone who knew the whole system thoroughly.

Putting the whole thing back together again and finding the way back to one's starting-point are not easy things to accomplish. This is why it is sometimes a good idea to call on the advice of those who have some expertise in this field, for example the SEEDS organisation. They will provide help for every stage of exploring the complexities of how creative worship works.

Earlier on I pointed out that it wasn't obligatory to dissect completely a service of worship in order to bring it to life again. Normally when cars break down they only need one or two elements looked at before they are back in working order again. But if a car has not had a service for a very long time then the chances are that it will need a fairly thorough overhaul. We don't tend to think of our services of worship needing a regular overhaul but we should.

A service of worship is a complicated mechanism which needs just as much looking after as a car. It certainly gets as much wear and tear as a car and we shouldn't expect it to be able to go on without a regular check-up. If our service of worship is in a fairly healthy state then the problem of isolating a particular element of the service that is not working properly is relatively simple. Like a doctor, we can put our finger on the sore spot, isolate it, look at it, repair it and replace it and all should be well. But have you ever noticed how when one thing goes wrong and it is repaired it is often not the end of the story? A whole series of additional complaints occur that need looking at. It really shouldn't surprise us because any fine piece of machinery works on principles of balance. When something goes wrong the whole focus of attention is centred on that weak spot but when the weak spot has been redressed it doesn't necessarily mean that all will be well again because the cause of the breakdown often lies at the heart of the machine.

A very interesting book came out some years ago called *Zen in the Art of Motor Cycle Maintenance*. One didn't need to know the first thing about how a motor cycle worked to learn from the book that when things go wrong we tend to look for the solutions at the point at which the thing has broken down. Does the machine purr smoothly as it should because if it doesn't there are liable to be a whole series of things that are out of kilter. How often do we listen to ourselves? We should because we can often sense what is wrong before it is too late and we need to go to a specialist for help.

Listening is a very important part of prayer. We can listen and God will tell us when things start to go off centre inside us. This is why a regular system of going on retreat is not only good for recharging the batteries of our soul but is essential for the maintenance of a healthy balance within us. So it is important to realise that, although we may think our worship is in fine fettle, it is wise to listen and take note every so often. If one element appears to be slightly out of harmony it may well be an indicator to future problems on a far greater scale. If major problems are discovered to be lurking underneath then it is important that full measures are taken to correct the malaise before a major breakdown occurs. Breakdowns take a terrible toll not only on their victims but on those who surround them. It is far wiser to nip the problems in the bud even though the repair work may appear to be expensive and time consuming.

But I don't want to mislead anyone, investigating the creative make-up of our worship is a serious undertaking that needs to be approached with all the care that goes into any major operation. The Gospels warn us that a person who builds his house on the sands or a king who goes to war without first considering the chances of his success is a fool. The life of our worship is a serious affair in that it gives us the backbone for our whole existence. To treat it as a necessary nuisance is folly. To think that it doesn't need careful consideration and regular check-ups is rash.

Perhaps it would be a good thing if the whole church family went away on retreat once a year specifically to check up on their regular services of worship. If the worship is alive and ticking over smoothly then the whole life of the church will flourish. For worship is the heartbeat of the church.

If the decision has been made to look at all stages of the worship then a major work has been undertaken and it is as well to plan very carefully for it. Before we embark on the project we need to know that we have a sufficient number of people in the church prepared to join in and stay the course. We need to plan the length of time we intend to spend on the project. Are we going to focus on one element each week? If that is the case the whole project will take about twelve to fourteen weeks. Sometimes we work best under pressure and given too much time we lose our concentration and reason for doing things. On the other hand it is unlikely that a group of people will be able to spend more than one evening a week on the project. Two to three hours per session is about right, but a lot of ground has to be covered.

Maybe your church needs to work more slowly and perhaps more thoroughly, and then a year would make better sense. Each month an element could be tackled at greater leisure with perhaps the whole of a Saturday devoted to the work. In this way you could keep it tied in to the whole process of worship. Work and research Saturday and see the results of your work on the Sunday. This would help you check that your creative research was providing results.

Whatever plan you choose it needs to be one that works for the majority of people who are participating. It needs to have that sense of fun and excitement about it that leads the congregation to want more.

The next question to ask ourselves is who is going to be in overall charge. The most obvious answer is the minister of the church but it doesn't have to be. There may be a valued member of the church who the minister feels would be ideal for the post. Clearly it needs to be someone with good, though unobtrusive, administrative skills. Someone who has caught the vision, can get things done, and can delegate effectively. Someone who has a sense of fun and is respected. But this is only the organiser of the project. You will also need people to lead each aspect of worship that is to be explored, people who have a particular artistic interest in which they can involve other people.

The list is pretty well endless from pottery to model making to sculpture to gardening, flower arranging, cooking, archery, car maintenance, hairdressing, photography, dressmaking, calligraphy as well as all the obvious arts such as dance, drama, music and painting. These people need to have caught the vision of what creative worship is about and how to use the questioning process to find the ways into experiencing worship through the use of the creative arts.

So we now have a team of people spearheaded by a leader who can keep the overall vision of the project in mind.

The next question to ask is whether everyone has a go at all the creative skills on offer, or whether a group stays with one and explores all the elements of worship through that art alone. The first option keeps everyone together but may well prove disruptive to real progress.

The second option works provided the leader can make sure that each group is working towards the common goal. If this option is used it is probably wise for the church to meet and share the fruits of their creativity by showing their work to each other and discussing the spiritual discoveries that have been made through it. Of course both options need space: either one large space or lots of small spaces which may be in the church, in people's homes or elsewhere. Ideally, they should be close enough for the leader to be able to move from place to place to observe the progress being made.

If careful preparation has been made at the beginning it is much easier for the leader of the project to bring all the stages of worship together at the end. It is wise to test out each stage as you go along and it is helpful to the health of the project if everyone participates. Then when it comes to the day of celebrating the whole of the renewed service it will not come as such a terrible shock, like the day of an exam when one can remember nothing of what one worked on at the beginning of the course.

Putting the whole thing together should come as a pleasant surprise. The surprise is in finding that the service works smoothly and easily, allowing everyone the ability to participate and re-explore the depths of meaning that are to be found in every stage of worship. This culminates in our being able to experience the power of celebration and outreach through a well understood and administered service. In achieving this we will have allowed the Spirit of God to act freely amongst us.

Do you know the story of the juggler who was found in a church juggling in front of the altar? When he was told that what he was doing was blasphemous and an insult to God he replied that it was the only way he knew how to thank God for all his goodness to him. The juggler was keeping his worship alive by practising his art before God.

He was celebrating his ability to give pleasure which was his way of reaching out to the world and he was thanking God for it. But his worship demanded a discipline of him. It was the discipline of being able to keep a number of clubs spinning in the air without them clattering to the floor.

We too need discipline in order to keep our services of worship alive. It is no good thinking that when we have researched all the reasons for our participating in every stage of our worship that we can then rest on our laurels in the belief that the process of worship will run itself. It won't. If we want our worship to remain alive we must continue to work at it. If we think that having asked questions about the stages of our worship and discovered some answers there are no more questions to be asked or answers found, we are fooling ourselves. If we think about our own lives we see that there is no point at which we can say we've got all the answers. In fact as we go on we find we know less and less but need to know more and more. This is the beginning of a healthy state of affairs because it gives us the chance to become more aware of the amazing sphere of God's unending creativity.

But we can only stay in this creative sphere if we are prepared to keep on asking questions and searching creatively for the answers. People who think there is no room for questioning have become fossilised. People who believe that to question things is wrong have become frightened of growth. People who deny the right of others to ask questions are those who have come to love power for its own sake. These people exist in the church as they do in every sphere of life, and they would, if they could, turn Christianity into a cult.

Christ shows us that we have to keep on learning if we wish to participate in the building of his Kingdom. When we keep on asking questions and searching for the answers we are keeping our worship of God alive. This life becomes real when we reach out to the world lovingly, in response to this worship. It isn't true that the process of asking questions upsets our belief in God. On the contrary it should strengthen our belief. There are people who will claim that questions lead us into error. But every moment of life poses questions which we have to answer. Movement is essential for life and movement involves us in this endless process of asking creative questions.

If you want life be brave enough to ask for it and the more you ask the more you'll receive. Keeping a service alive consists in knowing what is going on by continually asking questions. This keeps the various stages of worship revolving harmoniously like the juggler's clubs. It is the harmony of creative worship.

9

The Outcome

Moses strikes the rock in the desert and out comes living water. The Church is built on a rock. Jesus called Peter Cephas meaning a stone, a rock, and said, 'Upon this rock I will build my church' (Matt. 16:18). Peter who had showed all the signs of being like shifting sand eventually became a rock when he had finally grasped the true meaning of Christ's message. The rock is a sure foundation and it contains within it the abundant waters of life. If you live in an arid country you will understand how powerful the metaphor of water as a life-giving force is.

The Church is like the rock that Moses strikes. We are the Church and the rod with which we strike the rock is the urgency with which we approach our worship. Worship unlocks the waters of the spirit of life. All we have to do is to worship with all our heart, with all our mind, with all our soul and with all our strength. This is not difficult but it does demand all our attention and devotion if it is to provide us with the life that we long for, eternal and creative.

Christians believe that Christ was with God in the beginning. We believe that he appeared on earth, that he died, that he rose again to God and that he will come again. Through his sacrificial life we have eternal life. Note the element of sacrifice. Eternal life is assured us but only if we follow the truth which we find in Christ. The pattern of his sacrifice applies to us all. It doesn't mean that we have to suffer his crucifixion but it does mean that we have to be prepared to give away our creative life, which may feel like a crucifixion for us. But there is a paradox here. We are told that if we are prepared to give away our life we shall receive it back with eternal interest, and we are given the example of Jesus giving away his life so that others might live and yet receiving his life back again for ever.

Perhaps the aspect of Christianity that is actually the most difficult to believe in is the resurrection. We want to believe in it, we may think we do finally believe in it but the test of our belief will come when we are asked to sacrifice the thing we most want and love in life, whatever that may be. That test comes to everyone in varying ways irrespective of their beliefs. How do we respond? For Abraham the major test was one that paralleled the sacrifice of God. God wanted to know if Abraham loved him more than his own son. But he left the decision up to Abraham. Abraham's decision must have felt like a most terrible crucifixion and yet he was prepared to sacrifice what must have seemed to him to be his very own life. God shows us that he is prepared to make that sacrifice because although it must have felt as though he was crucifying himself yet he wanted life to come out of the rock of his faith.

This is the path that we are also asked to follow if we care about the life of the world as God cares about it. If our desire to worship God in church is a selfish one, one that we want to keep to ourselves then we shall live in empty churches with nothing but the empty echo of our own voices to keep us company. However small our sacrifice, however insignificant it may be, it must cost us everything like the widow's two mites put into the church coffers.

We cannot have everlasting creative life unless we are prepared to follow the pattern of our Saviour who in turn was showing us the pattern and the way of God himself. In John 16:19–24 Jesus is telling his disciples that he is about to leave them. It is a terrible moment for them. The grief of loss is combined with fear about an uncertain future. And yet he tells them that all this is necessary for them if they are to have eternal life. He tells them that his departure and their spiritual death will only last a short time before he returns to them in a different form. Then he will give back to them all the joy, mirth, love and zest for life that they had had when he was with them before.

We are no different to those disciples and the course of life and God's eternal plan have not changed. Their creative three-year period of worship with Jesus had come to an end. A new phase was about to begin. When it began at Pentecost those disciples burst onto an unsuspecting world with an energy, a fire and a passion that had never been seen before. They were accused of being drunk but in reality they had merely accepted the challenge of God's creative life which they knew they had to share with everyone they met. Such Christianity is within the grasp of every one of us today. Maybe not in so dynamic or dramatic a way but nevertheless in ways that will bring life and love, truth and joy, peace and goodwill flooding back into the world.

This world is hungry and thirsty for truth. It is tired of lies, deceit and double dealing and is anxious about its future. We as Christians through striking the rock of our faith with the devotion of our worship can, if we so desire, unleash the water of life to a thirsty world. We are the instruments, we are God's servants. But are we prepared to make the sacrifice of being creative vessels through which God can work his miracles in the world?

A Note on SEEDS

The SEEDS organisation was founded in 1982 in response to a need for a renewed spirit of creativity in the Church. It was the brainchild of the Revd Michael Farmery and his wife Margaret whose vision was to bring professional artists who were also Christians into the Church to encourage creativity within it.

Since that time SEEDS artists have held workshops in churches and with people of all denominations throughout the country. The artists themselves come from many different Christian backgrounds, but they share the same understanding of the vital role that creative disciplines can play in reviving liturgy and energising worship.

SEEDS has worked with individual church groups, or with individuals from various churches. It has also worked in schools, prisons, theological colleges, retreat houses and with ministers in post ordination training and mid-service training groups. It aims to serve the church as a whole and not one section of it. The expertise of its members covers a field as wide as that of creativity itself, from theatre to music, film and video to journalism, communication and counselling skills. It is a resource service which puts itself at the service of the church in both a training and consultative capacity.

If you would like further information on SEEDS please contact: SEEDS, 51 Pole Barn Lane, Frinton-on-Sea, Essex CO13 9AQ